RAND

A System Description of the Marijuana Trade

Michael Childress

Prepared for the
United States Army
RAND's Drug Policy Research Center

Arroyo Center
Drug Policy Research Center

Preface

This report describes and discusses applications for a computer spreadsheet–based, comprehensive "system description" of the quantity and flow of marijuana from cultivation, through international transportation, to domestic distribution, and ultimately to consumption. RAND has developed and documented similar system descriptions for cocaine and heroin. This effort is jointly sponsored by RAND's Arroyo Center and Drug Policy Research Center. This study should interest policymakers and analysts supporting the National Drug Control Program at the national level and others involved in resource allocation for, or analysis of, the drug problem.

The Arroyo Center

The Arroyo Center is the U.S. Army's federally funded research and development center (FFRDC) for studies and analysis operated by RAND. The Arroyo Center provides the Army with objective, independent analytic research on major policy and organizational concerns, emphasizing mid- and long-term problems. Its research is carried out in four programs: Strategy and Doctrine, Force Development and Technology, Military Logistics, and Manpower and Training.

Army Regulation 5-21 contains basic policy for the conduct of the Arroyo Center. The Army provides continuing guidance and oversight through the Arroyo Center Policy Committee (ACPC), which is co-chaired by the Vice Chief of Staff and by the Assistant Secretary for Research, Development, and Acquisition. Arroyo Center work is performed under contract MDA903-91-C-0006.

The Arroyo Center is housed in RAND's Army Research Division. RAND is a private, nonprofit institution that conducts analytic research on a wide range of public policy matters affecting the nation's security and welfare.

James T. Quinlivan is Vice President for the Army Research Division and Director of the Arroyo Center. Those interested in further information about the Arroyo Center should contact his office directly:

James T. Quinlivan
RAND
1700 Main Street
P.O. Box 2138
Santa Monica, CA 90407-2138

The Drug Policy Research Center

The Drug Policy Research Center (DPRC) is supported by the Ford and Weingart foundations. This work is part of the Center's extensive and ongoing assessment of drug problems at local and national levels. Audrey Burnam and Jonathan Caulkins are the co-directors of the DPRC. Those interested in further information about the DPRC should contact their offices directly. Audrey Burnam may be contacted at the above address; Jonathan Caulkins may be contacted at the following address:

RAND
2100 M Street, NW
Washington, DC 20037-1270

Contents

Figures

Tables

Summary

The United States has devoted substantial resources toward stemming the flow of illegal drugs. Yet it is difficult to accurately characterize the drug system, given that the production and trafficking of drugs are illegal enterprises cloaked in secrecy. While it is generally not possible to validate the basic parameters of the drug trade, a better understanding may help policymakers, law enforcement agencies, and analysts to evaluate and execute effective responses to the drug problem.

Purpose

A comprehensive accounting framework for estimating the quantities and flows of drugs would go a long way toward providing that understanding. To this end, RAND has developed—and this report documents—a computer spreadsheet–based "system description" of the quantity and flow of marijuana from cultivation, through international transportation, to domestic distribution, and ultimately to consumption. This system description can serve as a database and an analytical tool. It consists of four interrelated spreadsheets—a database and three others that mirror the general pattern of the marijuana trade: production, transportation, and U.S. distribution. The database provides primarily production related data from 1985 through 1991. This report provides user information for the model. The spreadsheets are available for either IBM (DOS) or Apple-based machines upon request to RAND.

Approach and Application

Using information available in the open literature, we constructed an end-to-end description of the marijuana trade with an emphasis on quantities entering the United States. Despite the fact that data are limited, we are able to tell a reasonably comprehensive story. The system framework allowed us (and any other user) to pool information from various sources while imposing consistency on these disparate data.

To examine the potential utility of this tool, this report examines three distinct but related applications: improving the estimation processes, conducting sensitivity analyses, and guiding planning and assessment. In improving the estimation process, an analyst can use the comprehensive framework to evaluate assumptions or data in terms of their downstream effects on other indicators. For example, it is possible to determine the likely effects of an increase in the marijuana crop yields. Sensitivity analysis can be used both to understand the import of certain parameters versus others (this may be helpful in allocating intelligence resources, for example) and to evaluate the first-order effects of change in the system, such as an eradication program.

Acknowledgments

The author is grateful to RAND colleagues Bonnie Dombey-Moore, Susan
Resetar, and Peter Reuter who, through their research on the cocaine system,
paved the way and made the author's work much easier. David Boyum
provided a thoughtful and comprehensive review, and Deborah Elms assisted in
document preparation.

1. Introduction

Background

The priority afforded to reducing illegal drug use in the United States increased considerably during the 1980s. This emphasis is evidenced by federal spending on anti-drug efforts, which increased from $1.5 billion in 1981 to a projected $12.7 billion in 1993, an increase of nearly 750 percent.[1] There have also been large increases in funding directed exclusively at quashing the marijuana trade, with federal spending doubling in 1991 to $35 million and requests for $87 million in 1992.[2] However, even this increase in federal expenditures may present only a partial picture, because some previously purchased resources have also been shifted to the drug war. The U.S. military's increasing role in antidrug efforts is a prime example.

The foundation of the U.S. military's involvement in the drug war was laid in 1981 when Congress amended the *Posse Comitatus* Act of 1878, paving the way for the military to assist civilian law enforcement agencies in the drug war.[3] By the late 1980s, illegal drug trafficking was declared a threat to U.S. national security,[4] and Congress had expanded the military's role in the drug war by mandating that the Department of Defense (DoD) play a leading role in at least four broad areas: (1) equipment loans; (2) training of law enforcement agency officials; (3) radar coverage of major drug trafficking routes; and (4) intelligence gathering and dissemination.[5]

Despite all the resources dedicated to stemming the illegal flow of drugs, the basic data and analytical tools available to decisionmakers have important gaps and limitations. For example, the government neither systematically estimates basic quantities of drug consumption nor provides systematic estimates of such

---

[1]*National Drug Control Strategy: Implementing the President's Plan*, Office of National Drug Control Policy, June 1992, p. 8. There was nearly a 400-percent increase from 1981 to 1989. See Carpenter and Rouse (1990), p. 2.

[2]Treaster (1991).

[3]The *Posse Comitatus* Act of 1878 prohibited the use of the military for civilian law enforcement. See U.S. Congress (1981).

[4]President Reagan signed a National Security Decision Directive (NSDD) in April of 1986 stating that the drug trade is a threat to U.S. national security. See Richburg (1986).

[5]U.S. General Accounting Office (1987), p. 2.

factors as domestic marijuana production. Under these circumstances, it becomes highly problematic to assess the impacts of different drug control programs.

Limitations of Current Information About the Drug Trade

The inadequacies of current data on the production, transportation, and consumption of illegal drugs frustrate analysts and policymakers alike in their attempts to understand the rudiments of illegal drug activities. It will always be difficult to obtain good data on an inherently clandestine activity. Complicating matters further, unlike heroin and cocaine, there is substantial domestic production of marijuana.[6] Deriving credible estimates of domestic marijuana production has proven to be as elusive as deriving credible estimates of foreign production. These data problems exacerbate the difficulty of making reasonable choices about how to allocate the scarce resources directed at reducing illegal drug use and complicate the task of measuring the effectiveness of chosen policies.

The two major sources of unclassified production data are the *International Narcotics Control Strategy Report* (INCSR), produced by the U.S. State Department's Bureau of International Narcotics Matters (INM), and *The NNICC Report* (formerly published as *The Narcotics Intelligence Estimate, NIE*), generated by an interagency group headed by the Drug Enforcement Agency (DEA).[7]

Basic production estimates from these documents, like estimates of marijuana production, have shown persistent differences.[8] Figure 1.1 shows the high and low estimates from the INCSR and NNICC from 1984 to 1989.[9]

The NNICC estimates have been consistently higher than the INCSR estimates for opium and coca production, but this is not the case with marijuana.[10] The INCSR's "high" estimate was higher than the NNICC's "high" estimate from

---

[6]Domestically grown marijuana has been estimated by various agencies to constitute from 12 to 35 percent of the U.S. market share.

[7]The NNICC Report is produced by the National Narcotics Intelligence Consumers Committee (NNICC).

[8]In 1990 the NNICC began publishing the INCSR numbers as the formal government estimate. However, there are still fundamental disagreements within and between these two groups (interview with a Defense Intelligence Agency analyst, May 1992).

[9]These estimates are for the major producers of marijuana (as opposed to hashish, another by-product of cannabis), which include Mexico, Colombia, Jamaica, and Belize. It includes an additional amount identified only as "other" in the INCSR and NNICC reports (probably from South America or Southeast Asia).

[10]See Childress (forthcoming).

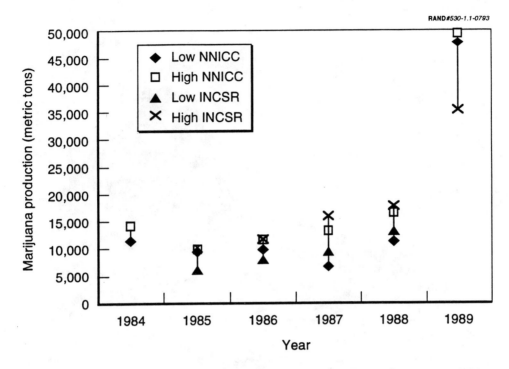

RAND#530-1.1-0793

Figure 1.1—Marijuana Production: NNICC and INCSR Estimates from 1984 to 1989

1986 through 1989. The wide range depicted in the figure for 1989 reflects a significant difference between the midpoints of the revised NNICC and INCSR estimates; the NNICC's midpoint is almost 40 percent higher than the INCSR's midpoint. The differences between the midpoints for other years have not been as dramatic, but still averaged 14 percent. The smallest difference occurred in 1986, when the NNICC midpoint was 6.8 percent higher than the INCSR, and the largest was in 1985, when the NNICC was 22.7 percent higher. (In 1987 and 1988, the INCSR was 22.7 and 10.5 percent higher, respectively.)

The uncertainties about marijuana production estimates compound the difficulty of determining marijuana consumption in the United States. For example, as shown in Figure 1.2, worldwide marijuana production increased steadily from 1985 to 1989 but then experienced a sharp downturn from 1989 to 1991.[11] The downturn since 1989 is mainly the result of a decrease in Mexican cannabis

---

[11]The estimated worldwide marijuana production is generated by the spreadsheet model described in this report. This model takes into account marijuana production by the world's major producers: Mexico, Colombia, Belize, and Jamaica. An estimate of (net) marijuana after losses, seizures, and consumption within the producing country is generated by the model. Added to this net production are the published estimates of "other" and U.S. domestic production (midpoints are used when a range is reported). The steep increase for Mexico in 1989 is based on improved estimating techniques and technologies. As a result, all estimates for Mexico prior to 1989 are generally believed to be incorrect.

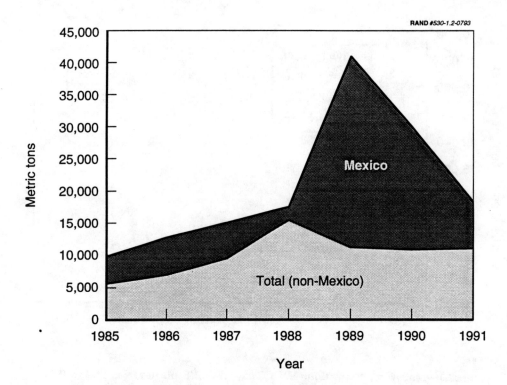

Figure 1.2—Estimated Worldwide Marijuana Production

cultivation (down 50 percent from 1989 to 1991) and an increase in Mexican cannabis eradication (up 170 percent from 1989 to 1991). The overall trend from 1985 to 1991, nevertheless, is one of steady increase, from 10,000 metric tons in 1985 to 18,000 metric tons in 1991. Likewise, even when Mexican production is removed from consideration, the overall trend from 1985 to 1991 is upward, from about 5,700 metric tons in 1985 to around 11,000 metric tons in 1991.

At the same time, domestic marijuana consumption figures do not reflect an increase in usage. While marijuana is still the most widely used illicit drug in the United States,[12] it has lost much of its social acceptability.[13] Indeed, as Figure 1.3 shows, the percentage of 18 to 25 years old who report smoking marijuana steadily decreased during the 1980s.[14] Also, the number of high school seniors

---

[12]Almost 10 million Americans are estimated to be current users (within the last 30 days) of marijuana. By comparison, the second most widely used illicit drug is cocaine, which reportedly has about 1.8 million current users, about one-fifth the number of marijuana users. See the U.S. Department of Health and Human Services (1991).

[13]Treaster (1991).

[14]These data are from National Institute on Drug Abuse (NIDA), National Household Survey on Drug Abuse for the 18 to 25 age group. The overall trend (i.e., 12 years old and older) is similar. See, for example, the U.S. Department of Health and Human Services (1991). The categories of "last year" and "last month" indicate that the individual used marijuana at least once during the specified time period.

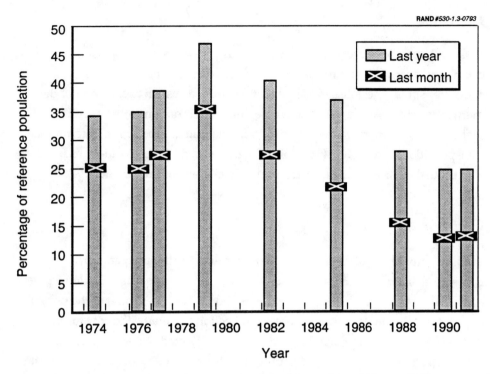

Figure 1.3—Marijuana Usage in the United States (18 to 25 Years Old)

who indicated that they did *not* disapprove of occasional marijuana use declined 30 percent from 1988 to 1990 (as reflected in the High School Senior Survey).[15]

Given the uncertainty that surrounds basic data on the marijuana trade, it is not surprising that sometimes there are vastly different estimates for the same factor, or that estimates for two different factors appear to be incompatible. The model described in this report can be used as a tool to help address these problems.

Since the drug trade is a "system," it is impossible to end up with more marijuana than the sum of the raw materials used in production.[16] By economic reasoning, there should also be some relationship between the prevalence or the amount of marijuana consumed and the amount produced. The system description imposes a framework that can enforce consistency in assumptions or data or, alternatively, can highlight sources of inconsistency. Essentially, it is an elaborate accounting scheme for reconciling estimates of the quantities and flows of marijuana.

---

[15]The White House, *National Drug Control Strategy*, January 1992, p. 27.

[16]This is meant as a general statement. If one is specifying a particular time period, some final product could come from storage and not from the raw materials of that period.

Purpose

This study provides decisionmakers and analysts with a tool to assist in estimating quantities and in charting the flow of marijuana. The tool is a computer spreadsheet–based model that provides a system description of the marijuana trade. Along with a database, the model contains other spreadsheets that mirror the general pattern of the marijuana trade: production, international transportation, and U.S. distribution. The model is designed to allow users to substitute data or to change the assumptions made about parameters.[17]

Outline

Section 2 provides a narrative account of marijuana cultivation and production. It describes the underlying process modeled in the spreadsheets. Section 3 gives a general system overview of the model; Section 4 discusses some of the possible applications the model could support; and Section 5 contains the conclusions. Appendix A lists the regional organization of the United States used in the spreadsheets; Appendices B and C provide more detailed information about the structure and operation of the spreadsheet model; Appendix D presents a short primer on the INCSR's data-collection methodology; and Appendix E displays the output from a simulation to test for the effect of propagating errors in the model.

---

[17]We have developed similar system descriptions for cocaine and heroin. See Childress (forthcoming) and Dombey-Moore, Resetar, and Childress (forthcoming).

2. The Marijuana Production Process

This section provides a brief overview of the marijuana production and transportation processes that underlie the spreadsheet model. It describes the steps in the process and some of the uncertainties surrounding production factors. It also summarizes the roles of various countries in the production and transportation of marijuana.

The first subsection provides a generic description of how marijuana is produced, but the description is notional in the sense that it does not take into account production differences that may occur in any of the marijuana-producing countries. The second subsection describes the uncertainty in some basic estimates of marijuana production.

Producing Marijuana

How Is It Done?

Marijuana, a by-product of the *Cannabis sativa L.* plant, is the most commonly used illicit drug in the United States. Its wide use can be partially attributed to the hardiness of the plant, which can be grown in a variety of temperate regions, including any one of the fifty American states. Compared to the production of heroin or cocaine, the processing of marijuana is extremely simple. Basically the plant is harvested, dried, and then smoked.

The cannabis plant is an annual grown from seed planted in the spring and is usually harvested once a year, typically in the fall. However, under ideal growing circumstances, it is possible to harvest two crops a year.[1] The marijuana is harvested by cutting down the plants, and then hanging them upside down until dry. After the plant has dried sufficiently, the largest stalks and stems are discarded. The remainder, which includes the leaves, seeds, flowers, and small stems, are combined and then sold as ordinary marijuana. This so-called commercial-grade or ordinary marijuana constitutes the bulk of the U.S. market.

---

[1]See U.S. Department of Defense (1987), p. 46.

A variation on this method produces Sinsemilla. Due to its higher THC content, Sinsemilla is more potent and expensive than commercial-grade marijuana.[2] Since the highest concentration of THC is found in the "buds" or unpollinated floral clusters, growers use semi-sophisticated agronomic techniques to maximize the size of the potent clusters. This increase is accomplished by eliminating all the male plants early in the growing season. The female plant responds to the lack of pollination by increasing the size of its buds to acquire the nonexistent pollen. These plants are harvested similarly to commercial-grade marijuana, but typically only the resin-rich buds are retained. The buds are "manicured" by trimming them of extraneous leaves and stems. The remainder of the plant is discarded, sold as commercial-grade marijuana, or used in the production of hashish.

Hashish, which has a THC content similar to commercial-grade marijuana, is produced by extracting the resins from buds, usually by shaking or rubbing, and then compressing the resins into a mass. Hash oil, yet another variation and the only product derived from the cannabis plant that involves synthetic chemicals, is a dark-colored substance made by removing the resins with a solvent. However, hashish users represent an extremely small percentage of the cannabis user population in the United States.[3] Hash use is much more prevalent in Europe, the Middle East, and Asia.

Who Does What?

The cannabis plant is grown in several countries. The principal marijuana producing countries that supply the U.S. market are Mexico, Colombia, Jamaica, and Belize. Significant production also occurs within the United States, and it is widely believed that only a minuscule amount is exported (most is consumed in the United States). In addition to these countries, substantial amounts of marijuana are grown in Brazil, Paraguay, Thailand, Laos, the Philippines, Cambodia, Australia, Burma, Indonesia, and Malaysia. However, it is believed that only small amounts of the marijuana grown in these countries ultimately find their way into the United States.[4] Substantial cannabis acreage can also be

---

[2]Delta-9 tetrahydrocannabinol (THC) is the primary psychoactive chemical in marijuana. Sinsemilla has typical THC levels of around 7 to 8 percent, which is considerably higher than the 2 to 3 percent found in most commercial grades. See *The NNICC Report, 1990* (1991), p. 30.

[3]Ibid.

[4]It is believed that most of the marijuana crop in Brazil and Paraguay is consumed locally or shipped to other South American and European countries. Less is known about the status of marijuana production in the other countries, but in recent years the Southeast Asian countries of Thailand and Laos have emerged as exporters of marijuana to the United States. Indeed, these countries are usually aggregated into the "other" category, and are estimated to account collectively for around 10 percent of the U.S. market. See *The NNICC Report 1990* (1991), pp. 35–37.

found in Lebanon, Pakistan, Afghanistan, and Morocco, but ostensibly most of this cannabis is converted to hash, which is generally consumed in the Middle East and Europe.[5]

Figure 2.1 shows the estimated marijuana production (in metric tons) for the principal suppliers to the United States.[6] The steep increase for Mexico in 1989 is based on improved estimating techniques and technologies. As a result, all estimates for Mexico prior to 1989 are generally believed to be incorrect.[7] It is not obvious which countries are included in the "other" category from reading the INCSR and NNICC reports, but this category probably includes Brazil, Paraguay, Thailand, and Laos.

Figure 2.2 shows the relative distribution of the major suppliers to the United States. Mexico is believed to supply nearly 70 percent of the marijuana in the

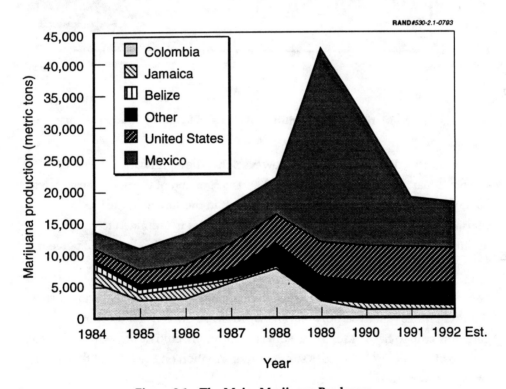

Figure 2.1—The Major Marijuana Producers

---

[5]According to the INCSR, March 1992, the data for Pakistan and Afghanistan are virtually nonexistent, but most cannabis is processed into hash. There are data for Lebanon and Morocco (the world's largest grower of cannabis), but the assumption is that all cannabis produced in these countries is converted to hash and shipped to the Middle East and Europe.

[6]The estimated marijuana production presented in Figure 2.1 is generated by the spreadsheet model described in this report. These estimates are based on cultivation estimates found in various editions of the INCSR and NNICC reports.

[7]See Abt Associates (1991), p. 39.

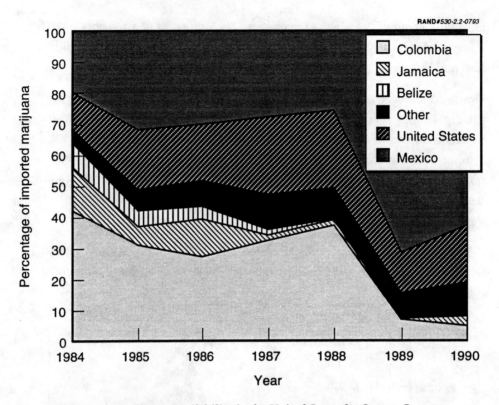

RAND#530-2.2-0793

Figure 2.2—Marijuana Availability in the United States by Source Country

United States.[8] It should be noted, however, that the significant increase of Mexico's market share since the mid-1980s is a function of the revised estimates as noted above rather than a fundamental shift in the source of the U.S.'s marijuana. Marijuana produced in the United States is estimated to comprise about 20 percent of the U.S. market from 1984 to 1990, with a low of 12 percent in 1984 and a high of 25 percent in 1988.[9]

Several countries are involved in the marijuana trade, and they play varied roles. Some countries mainly supply marijuana, while others convert most of their cannabis crop to hash. Moreover, some countries are cultivators, while others are transit sites. Table 2.1 provides summary information on the roles of the principal countries.

---

[8]These percentages are found in various editions of the NNICC reports.

[9]These are the estimates published in the annual NNICC reports. Other agencies have offered different estimates.

Table 2.1

Illicit Cannabis Trade Countries at a Glance

Country	Primary Roles	Primary Product	Eradication	Use
Afghanistan	Cultivation	Hashish	None	Unknown
Belize	Cultivation	Marijuana	Yes[a]	10,000 users/10 metric tons
Brazil	Cultivation	Marijuana	Yes	Widespread[b]
Colombia	Cultivation	Marijuana	Yes[c]	Rough est. of 2 metric tons
Dominican Rep.	Transit	Marijuana	n.a.	Unknown[d]
Jamaica	Cultivation, transit	Marijuana	Yes[e]	Unknown
Laos	Cultivation, transit	Marijuana	Unknown	Unknown
Lebanon	Cultivation	Hashish	None	Unknown
Mexico	Cultivation, transit	Marijuana	Yes	Low
Morocco	Cultivation	Hashish	Minimal[f]	20 to 70% of population
Pakistan	Cultivation	Hashish	Yes	Est. 1,000,000
Paraguay	Cultivation	Marijuana	Yes	Unknown[b]
Philippines	Cultivation, Transit	Marijuana	Yes	Unknown
Thailand	Cultivation	Marijuana	Yes	Unknown
The Bahamas	Transit	Marijuana	n.a.	Negligible
United States	Cultivation	Marijuana	Yes	10 to 20 million[g]

[a]About 80 percent of the cultivated hectares have been eradicated each year since 1988.

[b]It is believed that much of the marijuana grown in Brazil and Paraguay is consumed in Brazil.

[c]The number of hectares under cultivation is about one-fourth of what it was just a few years ago.

[d]The 1992 INCSR reports that there are 170,000 cocaine/marijuana users in the Dominican Republic.

[e]About 50 percent of the cultivated hectares were eradicated each year since 1988.

[f]An estimated 0.1 percent of the hectares were eradicated in 1991.

[g]The 1991 National Household Survey found that about 10 million are current users (within last 30 days) with an additional 10 million using marijuana within the last year.

Uncertainty on Production Estimates

Basic information on foreign marijuana production, such as the number of hectares under cultivation, the level of indigenous marijuana consumption, or the amount exported to the United States, is difficult to obtain. Consequently, considerable uncertainty surrounds many of the basic estimates on marijuana production. This is as true of domestic production as it is for foreign production. As discussed in Section 1, the two principal U.S. government agencies charged with estimating the number of hectares under cultivation and gross marijuana production frequently do not concur. Here, disagreements are especially troublesome, since the number of hectares under cultivation can be obtained through aerial and satellite surveillance and is therefore thought to be the most reliable of the basic estimates.

However, even with the aid of such technology, estimating the number of hectares under cultivation has been likened to finding a needle in a haystack. The four major suppliers of marijuana to the U.S.—Belize, Colombia, Jamaica, and Mexico—have a total land area of 1,214,446 square miles but reportedly need only 137 square miles to grow all their export marijuana.[10] The analogy holds for other drugs as well and, in some cases, is even more extreme.[11]

And, for many marijuana-producing countries, no production estimates are offered at all. The 1990 NNICC Report says that

> In the late 1980s, Southeast Asia emerged as a major exporter of marijuana to the United States. Most of the marijuana destined for the United States comes from Thailand and Laos, and, to a lesser extent, the Philippines and Cambodia. Other nations such as Australia, Burma, Indonesia, Malaysia, some of the Pacific islands, and Vietnam also produce marijuana. *However, the extent of cultivation and ultimate export are not known for these countries. As a result, specific figures are unavailable for 1990.*[12] (italics added)

Another indication of the uncertainty that surrounds the estimation process is the occasional revision of the published data from year to year. The revision to the Mexican marijuana production estimate in the late 1980s is perhaps the most notable example of changing estimates. Improved survey technologies, not increased cultivation, are thought to account for the increase in Mexico's hectares (ha) of marijuana from 1988 (9,000 ha) to 1989 (58,000 ha).[13] This increase in the cultivation estimate led to a revision in Mexico's marijuana production estimate for 1989 from 4,750 metric tons[14] to 30,200 metric tons.[15] However, there have been other revisions in the Mexican estimates, if somewhat less dramatic.[16] For example, as a result of additional information from the Government of Mexico, the estimate of marijuana eradicated in 1989 was lowered in later publications,[17]

---

[10]U.S. Department of Defense (1987), p. 68.

[11]See Dombey-Moore, Resetar, and Childress (forthcoming) and Childress (forthcoming).

[12]*The NNICC Report, 1990* (1991), p. 37.

[13]*The NNICC Report 1989* (1990), p. 65.

[14]*INCSR*, Department of State (March 1989), p. 113.

[15]*INCSR* (March 1992), p. 177.

[16]The many revisions in Mexican production estimates are probably a function of greater attention, given Mexico's dominance of the U.S. market. So the lack of revisions to the estimates for other countries is probably not an indication of greater confidence in those estimates.

[17]*INCSR*, 1992, pp. 177–178.

and the estimated yield per hectare was further refined.[18] The difficulty of obtaining reliable information on a country that is contiguous with the United States and that is its principal foreign supplier of marijuana implies even more uncertainty in estimates for countries that ostensibly play a less important role vis-à-vis the United States.

Other estimates seem equally fragile. For instance, a "loss factor" is commonly assigned to a country's production to account for any losses that might occur during cultivation and harvesting, but it is not clear how these estimates are determined or why they are assigned selectively. For example, Belize is charged with a "loss factor" of 5 percent, but Mexico, Colombia, and Jamaica have none.[19] As a result, these factors appear somewhat arbitrary.

It is also difficult to accurately estimate the amount of marijuana consumption in the producing states, as evidenced by the INCSR's "rough estimate" for Colombian marijuana consumption.[20] And the U.S. is often dependent on the governments of producing countries—which are sometimes alleged to be rife with corruption—for such basic information as seizure data.

Given the uncertainty in estimates, it is common for both low- and high-end estimates to be offered representing a wide range, instead of a narrow range or a point estimate (as discussed in Section 1). We have discussed aggregate NNICC and INCSR estimates; obviously, these aggregate differences can translate into significant differences at the country level. Some of these differences are illustrated in Table 2.2.

This discussion has highlighted many inconsistencies and uncertainties associated with basic factors of the marijuana system. Under these circumstances, fundamental estimates, such as the amount produced, the amount consumed in country, the quantity lost during production, or the amount shipped to the United States, may be unreliable.

---

[18]Before 1990, the usable plant yield was inadequately estimated. However, according to the 1992 INCSR, in 1990 "information from the Government of Mexico officials has enabled us to obtain a more accurate understanding of the actual amount of usable plant yield versus whole plant yield," p. 178. This resulted in a reduction of the yield factor from over 1.0 to about 0.5 metric tons per hectare.

[19]INCSR, 1992.

[20]INCSR, 1992, p. 110.

Table 2.2

A Comparison of Marijuana Production Estimates for 1989

	Mexico	Colombia	Jamaica	Belize	Domestic	Other
INCSR (mt)	29,688	1,088	279	59.4	n.a.	3,000–4,000
NNICC (mt)	42,283	2,300	142	56	5,000–6,000	3,000–5,000
Difference (%)	42.4	111.4	96.5	6.1	n.a.	14.3

NOTE: The NNICC estimates are from the 1989 report. The INCSR estimates for Colombia, Jamaica, Belize, and Other are from the 1989 report, but the Mexico estimate is from the 1991 INSCR Report. This is because, unlike the 1989 NNICC Report, the 1989 INCSR Report does not reflect the adjusted Mexico estimates. Both sets of numbers reflect net production (i.e., after in-country seizures and consumption). The midrange value is used to calculate the percentage difference when a range is provided.

3. Overview of the System Description

RAND has developed a series of computer-based spreadsheets to model the marijuana production process described in the previous section. We label these spreadsheets in the aggregate a system description, and this section provides a general overview. The system description consists of four related spreadsheets, which together can serve both as a database and analytical tool. We designed flexibility into the system description so analysts can easily substitute data or modify assumptions.

Components of the System Description

While the specifics of drug industries may vary, each follows the same overall pattern, which provides the basis of our system description. Figure 3.1 describes the pattern and compares it with our system description components.

RAND#530-3.1-0793

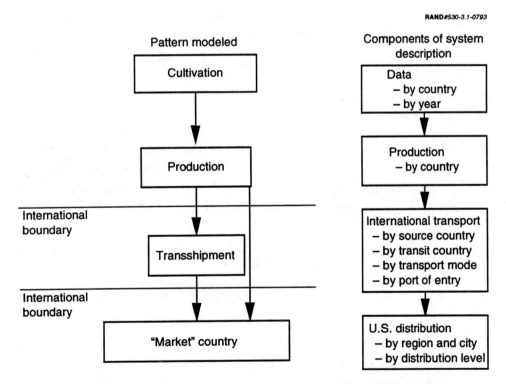

Figure 3.1—Pattern of Drug Flow Compared to System Description

The various activities or functions can be characterized as production, international transportation, and domestic distribution. For convenience then, each of these activities has a separate spreadsheet devoted to it.

Four computer-based spreadsheets form the system description for marijuana.[1] The first is a **Database** primarily of production-related data (from 1985 through 1991) that is linked to the system spreadsheets and can provide the initial conditions for the model.[2] Each record of the database provides data on a country's low and high values for a variety of production estimates. These data are taken from the open literature, primarily the INCSR and the NNICC reports.

Three system spreadsheets mirror the categories of activities noted above: **Production, International Transportation,** and **U.S. Distribution.** The spreadsheets model the flow of marijuana through the entire system for one year at a time; an extract from the database spreadsheet can provide the initial conditions for a given year, or the analyst can substitute others. The diagram on the right side of Figure 3.1 provides a schematic of the spreadsheet structure.

Production Spreadsheet

The production spreadsheet begins with an estimate of cultivated area and ends with an estimate of the amount of marijuana ready for shipment to the world's markets. It builds an estimate of marijuana using parameters for the amount of marijuana (in metric tons) per cultivated hectare and for each participating (or source) country. Losses due to seizures, consumption, or any other reason are accounted for in the spreadsheet.

Embedded graphs show the gross and net production for each producer country, and Figure 3.2 is an example of a summary graph that displays each country's "market share."[3] For example, Mexico's production clearly dominates the U.S. foreign supply of marijuana, while Belize's production is negligible.

International Transportation Spreadsheet

The international transportation spreadsheet takes the amount of marijuana ready for export from the production spreadsheet and generates an estimate of

---

[1]The software is Microsoft Excel, and the model can be made available for either PC or Macintosh hardware.

[2]The examples in this section are based on 1991 data.

[3]Net production is after consumption, seizures, and other losses are removed.

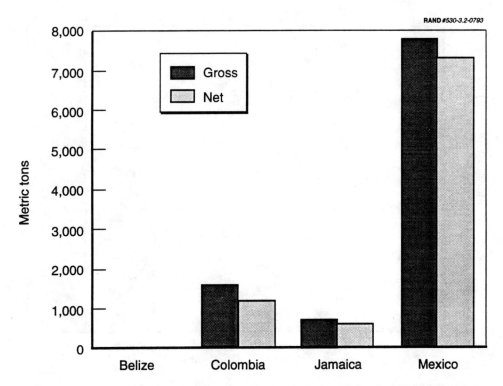

Figure 3.2—Estimated Marijuana Production by the U.S.'s Major Suppliers in 1991

the amount successfully smuggled into the United States according to user-determined transshipment parameters. It consists of a matrix that systematically divides the volume of marijuana from producer to transit countries; the matrix is then subdivided into other matrices that allocate the marijuana to the world's markets.[4] Still other matrices allocate the marijuana to U.S. regions by transportation mode. The spreadsheets have the capability to remove marijuana from the system because of foreign or domestic seizures at the point of entry into the United States. Again, built-in graphs, such as Figure 3.3, provide a variety of summary information.

All of the spreadsheet matrices are linked. One matrix takes the drug from the producer countries and distributes it to the shipping countries. For example, much of the marijuana produced in Colombia and Jamaica is shipped through the Bahamas and the Dominican Republic. A transshipment matrix in the marijuana international transportation spreadsheet allows the user to transfer the world's estimated marijuana production from country to country. A second

---

[4]We have included storage as a "market" from which product can be made available for a later year.

18

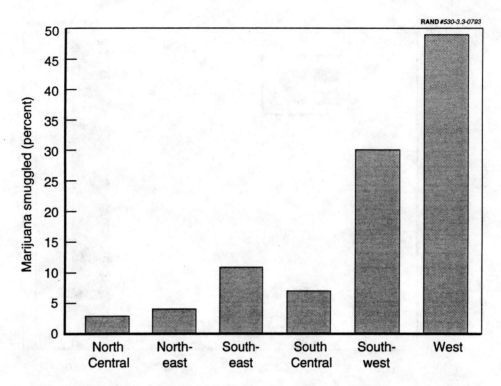

Figure 3.3—Estimated Distribution of Marijuana Smuggling by U.S. Entry Region

matrix takes the drug from the shipping countries and distributes it to the world's markets, including the United States. After foreign seizures are removed from the system, a third matrix allows the user to distribute the drug within the United States.

At this point in the system description, the United States has been divided into six regions (see Appendix A for a list of states composing each region). The sources of marijuana vary among the regions, as do the primary transportation modes. Another matrix defines the drug flow by transportation modes: private or commercial land, sea, or air. Thus, the spreadsheet shows, for example, that in 1991, the West region is estimated to have received much of its marijuana via commercial and private land transportation, while the Southeast got most of its marijuana via commercial and private sea transportation. The final matrix operating in this spreadsheet accounts for seizures, i.e., drugs seized at the U.S. borders.

At various points in the system, the analyst can compare model outputs with exogenously derived estimates to evaluate how reasonable some parameter estimates are in terms of their effect on other parameters. For example, the model keeps a running tabulation of the source of the United States' marijuana, so it is possible to determine the relative percentages between the producing countries. This information can, in turn, be compared with the NNICC's data on the sources of the U.S. marijuana supply or other data in which an analyst has reasonably high confidence.

U.S. Distribution Spreadsheet

The final spreadsheet tracks the domestic distribution of drugs. It begins with the amount successfully smuggled into each of the U.S. entry regions and ends with an estimate of the total number of users in the United States. As with all of the spreadsheets, the analyst can substitute other estimates. A matrix is provided so the user can make interregional transfers and subtract losses—owing either to domestic law enforcement or other removals and inventory losses. Then, depending on what the analyst determines to be typical consumption levels, an estimate is generated of the number of users. This estimate can then be compared to the estimate from the National Household Survey on Drug Abuse, allowing the analyst to calibrate the model in another fashion.

Limitations

Limitations of the system description fall into two categories. The first is analytic; it is a description and takes behavior as given. Second, it rests on incomplete and often questionable data. Of course, this same weakness makes the system approach useful and, indeed, necessary.

The framework is not adaptive. By itself, it cannot provide information on how the system might change in response to policy choices or strategies. The following example illustrates this point. Suppose Thailand's marijuana production is reduced by 50 percent, and the analyst is interested in the impact this reduction will have on the level of marijuana entering the United States. The analyst can simply cut Thailand's marijuana production in half and see how much is entering the United States. However, this assumes that Thai (and other) traffickers behave similarly regardless of the level of production, when it is quite likely that they will behave differently. If the analyst has assumed that, for example, 5 percent of Thailand's marijuana crop is shipped to the United States, it is not necessarily the case that 5 percent will be shipped to the United States after production has been reduced by 50 percent. It is perhaps more likely that markets closer to home (and hence easier to supply) will be satiated first and, speaking hypothetically, there may be sufficient demand to absorb all of the remaining production. So the percentage shipped to the United States probably *interacts* with Thailand's total production. The model does not anticipate these interactions; it is the responsibility of the user to be cognizant of them. However, the model can incorporate findings from economic and/or behavioral models of particular sectors and show a first approximation of the systemwide effect of policies directed at those sectors.

Finally, the framework generally models drug flows in only one direction—from production through consumption. This means that if an analyst overrides the data in the international transportation spreadsheet, for example, the model will show the downstream implications of the analyst's estimates (i.e., the amount entering the United States and distributed in the United States), but it will not automatically show the upstream changes in production or processing estimates required to be consistent with the analyst's data. However, these types of problems can be explored by using Excel's Goalseeker or Solver function, allowing the user to derive the upstream estimates that would be consistent with changes in downstream data, albeit at a more aggregate level of detail.

4. Applications for the System Description

The system description has at least three distinct, but related, uses: improving the estimation process, sensitivity analysis, and planning and assessment.

Improving Estimation

There are significant inconsistencies between production and consumption estimates. Basic disagreements about whether the drug problem is improving or deteriorating would be at least partially resolved if it were possible to link indicators from different parts of the system. The system description forces consistency (which is not to be confused with accuracy or validity) on the estimation process.

There is abundant opportunity for the model to highlight inconsistencies among estimates of the marijuana system. To illustrate how the model can highlight and help resolve inconsistencies in estimates, we examine two important questions surrounding the marijuana trade:

- How much marijuana is consumed in the United States?
- How much marijuana is grown in the United States?

Estimating U.S. Marijuana Consumption

A number of sources provide different estimates of annual marijuana consumption or the current amount available for consumption in the United States. For example, a Congressional Research Service report indicates that U.S. consumption levels in 1988 were 6,000 to 9,000 metric tons (80 percent imported).[1] *The NNICC Report 1989* reports that the net marijuana available for U.S. consumption in 1988 was 12,130 to 16,710 metric tons,[2] but provides no

---

[1]Surrett (1988), p. 1.

[2]*The NNICC Report 1989*, p. 55. This range of values represents the net marijuana available in the United States *after* seizures within the producing country, consumption within the producing country, U.S. seizures (e.g., coastal, border, and internal—but not domestic eradication), seizures during shipment (e.g., those on the high seas, within transshipment countries, and from aircraft), and other losses (e.g., abandoned shipments, undistributed stockpiles, inefficient handling and transportation).

estimate of actual U.S. consumption. Nevertheless, if we take 75 percent of each of the values, we obtain an estimate of U.S. consumption that is between 9,098 and 12,533 metric tons.[3] The 1992 *INCSR* indicates that approximately 16,000 metric tons were available for consumption in the U.S. in 1988.[4] Again using the 75 percent figure, we obtain an estimate of U.S. consumption that is equal to 12,000 metric tons. These three sources provide two ranges and one point estimate that barely overlap each other. The range of values for potential U.S. marijuana consumption in 1988 goes from a low estimate of 6,000 metric tons to a high estimate of 12,000 metric tons, a 100 percent difference.

What is the analyst or policymaker to make of these estimates? Which of these estimates, if any, are plausible? The model can be used to help resolve these questions. For example, the National Household Survey on Drug Abuse estimated that approximately 21 million Americans used marijuana at least once during 1988 (12 million people had used the drug in the last 30 days, and 6.6 million in the last week). Assuming that this estimate of 21 million users is essentially correct, if average individual consumption is 72 grams per year,[5] then about 1,544 metric tons would be consumed—a level significantly lower than the previously cited estimates that ranged from 6,000 to 12,000 metric tons. If average annual user consumption is increased to 115 grams,[6] 2,447 metric tons would be consumed, and at 180 annual grams[7] the total U.S. consumption is still far below the 6,000 metric tons estimate at 3,812. If we average all of these

---

[3]The 75 percent estimate is admittedly somewhat arbitrary, but has precedent. In a report done for ONDCP, Abt Associates (1991) uses the 75 percent figure to generate an estimate of how much Mexican marijuana enters the United States (see p. 41). Also see *The NNICC Report, 1985–1986* (pp. 6–15). The estimate of U.S. consumption for 1985, 4,693.9 metric tons, which was provided by the National Institute on Drug Abuse, U.S. Department of Health and Human Services, is approximately 75 percent of the NNICC's 1985 lower estimate of net marijuana available for U.S. consumption, which ranged from 6,400 to 8,300 metric tons.

[4]*International Narcotics Control Strategy Report*, March 1992. This number represents the theoretical potential yield *minus* seizures and consumption within Mexico, Colombia, Jamaica, and Belize (no marijuana is subtracted for the 3,500 metric tons produced by "Other").

[5]The estimate of 72 grams per year is derived from work done by Abt Associates for the Office of National Drug Control Policy. Using the National Household Survey on Drug Abuse, Abt Associates estimated that average consumption was about 12 "joints" per month. Assuming that the average joint size is about 0.5 grams (see Abt Associates [1991], p. 15, fn. 17), this is 6 grams per month or 72 grams per year (Abt Associates, 1991, fn. 26).

[6]This estimate was offered by a statistician with the National Organization for the Reform of Marijuana Laws (NORML), a group that advocates the legalization of marijuana. The actual reported estimate is a quarter pound per year, which translates into 115 grams. See Warner (1986), p. 33.

[7]The ONDCP has estimated that an upper limit is about 15 grams per month, or 180 grams per year.

consumption estimates, we get 122 annual grams[8] or about 2,534 metric tons for 21 million users.[9]

Figure 4.1 illustrates these differences, and they are stark. The "supply-side" estimates offered by the CRS, NNICC, INCSR are much higher than the "demand-side" estimates derived from the National Household Survey based on the number of users and a reasonable range of consumption levels.[10]

Is there any way to reconcile these estimates? Obviously, the disparities are too large to reconcile all of them. But can we reconcile the CRS estimate of 6,000 metric tons with, for example, the estimate of 3,812 metric tons generated by the 180 grams per year assumption? For us to believe that 6,000 metric tons were

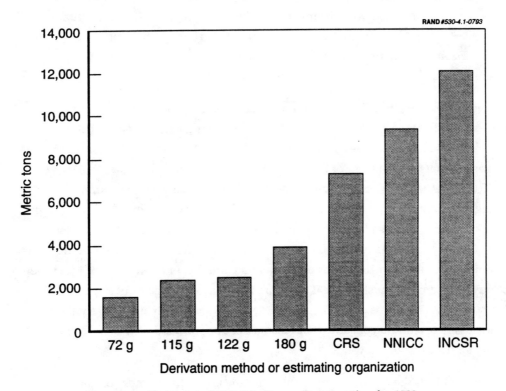

Figure 4.1—Estimates of U.S. Marijuana Consumption for 1988

---

[8]The estimate of 122 annual grams is similar to an estimate that was generated in another RAND project. An exploration of NIDA's National Household Survey on Drug Abuse data resulted in an estimate of about 100 grams per year. The estimated average consumption level of 100 grams per year accounts for the differences in consumption by heavy and light users. It does so by weighting the estimated number of users who reside in each of the Survey's marijuana consumption categories.

[9]The model is constructed to use a single average consumption level. Alternatively, others have generated separate estimates for light and heavy users based on the potency of the marijuana (i.e., THC content). See Kleiman (1989), pp. 37–39.

[10]The CRS estimate is the midpoint of the 6,000 to 9,000 range. The NNICC estimate of 9,098 is 75 percent of the lower range estimate, and the INCSR estimate of 12,000 is 75 percent of its point estimate.

consumed and that the average annual consumption level was 180 grams, there must have been about 33 million users—not 21 million users. The analyst must decide if this represents a reasonable error band around the National Household Survey estimates.[11] Alternatively, by holding the estimates of 6,000 metric tons and 21 million users constant, the average annual consumption level would have to be about 290 grams per year, which is about 580 joints annually or one-and-a-half joints per day. Again, the analyst must decide if this is a tenable assumption.

Estimating Domestic Marijuana Production

A CRS report in 1989 estimated that 25 to 35 percent of the marijuana consumed in the United States is domestically produced.[12] The NNICC reported that 13 percent was the accurate percentage for 1989, and estimated 18 percent for 1990.[13] The NNICC further estimated that 5,000 to 6,000 metric tons of marijuana were domestically produced in 1990 and that about 3,300 metric tons were eradicated.[14]

This leaves 1,700 to 2,700 metric tons of domestically produced marijuana available for consumption in 1990. If it is true that this much domestically produced marijuana was consumed in the United States and that it constituted approximately 18 percent of the total U.S. consumption,[15] it follows that 9,444 to 15,000 metric tons were consumed by Americans in that year—an extraordinarily high amount. Even if the percentage share of the market claimed by U.S.-grown marijuana is increased to 30 percent, the level of metric tons consumed is over 7,000. To accept this 7,000–metric ton estimate, 39 million Americans would need to use an average of 180 grams of marijuana annually, or an average of 1 joint per day. The analyst must decide if these are reasonable changes, but a twofold increase over NIDA's estimated number of users seems too high, especially when the average amount consumed represents the upper bound of what officials in the ONDCP believe is valid.

Most analysts seem fairly comfortable with the estimated number of marijuana users in the National Household Survey on Drug Abuse, and this figure is

---

[11]The 95-percent confidence intervals around the marijuana population usage estimates are typically quite narrow. For example, NIDA's National Household Survey on Drug Abuse estimate for Americans who used marijuana in 1988 is 21.1 million. The range of estimates reflecting the 95-percent confidence interval is 18.6 million to 23.9 million. Consequently, the 33 million users estimate does not approach the upper bound of this 95-percent confidence interval.

[12]Perl (1989), p. 2.

[13]*The NNICC Report 1990*, p. 34.

[14]*The NNICC Report 1990*, p. 31.

[15]It is generally assumed that no significant amount of domestically produced marijuana is exported.

approximately 20 million users for 1991. Moreover, the estimated average annual consumption level of 122 grams seems reasonable, since it constitutes, as an average, a typical usage pattern. Given these two estimates, about 2,500 metric tons were consumed by Americans in 1991, of which it is estimated that between 450 metric tons (18 percent of the market) and 875 metric tons (35 percent) were domestically produced. The midrange of these two values, 663 metric tons, is roughly *one-third* of the NNICC's estimate (1,700 to 2,700 metric tons) of U.S. domestic production available for consumption in 1990.

Sensitivity Analysis

Given the limitations of available data, one of the most important contributions of the model, aside from imposing a conditional framework on disparate sources of information, is the ability to perform parameter sensitivity analysis easily. For example, Table 4.1 illustrates the percentage change in the two output measures for a 50 percent increase in selected parameter values. For instance, by increasing Colombia's parameter estimate of marijuana (metric tons) per hectare by 50 percent, from 0.83 to 1.24, the model produces a 6-percent increase in the amount of marijuana shipped to the United States and a 3.9-percent increase in the estimated number of users.

Assuming all other things are equal, it is clear that changes in some parameters have a much greater impact on the system than changes in other parameters. This information can be useful for, among other things, allocating intelligence resources. If, for example, the estimated number of users in the United States is

Table 4.1

Sample Parameter Sensitivity Analysis

Parameters Increased	Marijuana Shipped to U.S.[a]	Estimated Number of Users[a]
Metric tons of marijuana per hectare		
Colombia	6.00	3.90
Jamaica	2.30	1.50
Mexico	28.20	18.30
Eradication area (ha)		
Colombia	0	0
Jamaica	−2.00	−1.30
Mexico	−17.00	−11.10
Mexico consumption (metric tons)	−0.40	−0.20
Foreign seizures	−0.04	−0.03
U.S. border seizures	−0.90	−0.60
Domestic production (metric tons)	n.a.	17.60
Annual consumption	n.a.	−33.30

[a]Percentage change for a 50-percent increase in parameter value.

increased by over 17 percent when the parameter for U.S. domestic production is changed by 50 percent, it would be highly important to get this estimate correct. By comparison, Mexican marijuana consumption and foreign seizures have a comparatively small impact on the outcome measures.

Analytic resources need to be allocated where they will produce the greatest returns. Resources might be focused on the most uncertain parameters, but also on the parameters that sensitivity analysis has shown to be critical in the determination of the flow of marijuana to the United States. Another consideration, of course, is the cost of attaining a given percentage reduction in the parameter uncertainty.

To evaluate whether resources are being allocated in a cost-effective fashion, it might be useful to compare current resource allocations with the results of a sensitivity analysis similar to the illustrative analysis shown in Table 4.1. If inordinate resources are being spent on determining the "correct" value of a parameter that a sensitivity analysis has shown to be relatively unimportant, an alternative allocation could be justified.

Planning and Assessment

Tracking regional flows serves a number of programmatic and analytic purposes. For instance, it can help the analyst focus attention on the consequences of an increase or decrease in production on the flows of traffic along different routes. We have estimated that all of the marijuana produced in Mexico enters the United States through the Southwest and West regions. Consequently, changes in Mexican production estimates will have differing implications for each region of the United States. As already explained, in 1989, the Mexican production estimate was revised substantially upward as a result of better intelligence. The resulting impact on the model's estimate of the level of illegal drug traffic is significant. Figure 4.2 shows the estimated percentage increase in commercial land drug flow by region when the Mexican marijuana production estimate is changed from the old (about 4,500 metric tons) to the new (around 30,000 metric tons) value. Radically different implications obviously result for planning and assessment.[16]

---

[16]This example of how the model can be used for planning and assessment purposes can also be used as an example of the model's limitations. In Section 3, we discussed the model's limitations, and one of the limitations we discussed is that the model is descriptive and not adaptive. As a result, *interactions* are not modeled. Without an explicit modification, all transportation modes, not just commercial land, would experience the same percentage increase, when in fact it is likely that there would be differential effects. For example, it is likely that there are preferred transportation modes and that, as production increases, these modes are used to a greater extent than others. Then, once a threshold is reached, other transportation modes begin to handle the excess production. Again, this is not automatically handled by the model, but the user can certainly change these estimates.

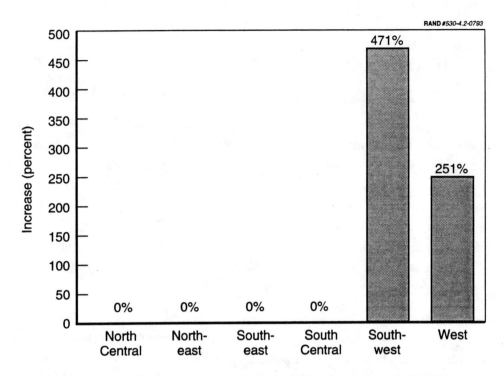

Figure 4.2—Estimated Percentage Increase in Drug Flow by Commercial Land from
Revision of Mexican Production Estimates

5. Conclusions

The amount of resources devoted to stemming the flow of illegal drugs into the United States is substantial, and yet considerable uncertainty surrounds the basic parameters of the drug system. This situation is understandable given that the production and trafficking of illegal drugs are generally conducted in secrecy. This also makes it extremely difficult to evaluate the accuracy of basic factors in the marijuana trade. Nevertheless, if policymakers, law enforcement agencies, and analysts are to promulgate, execute, and evaluate responses to the drug problem, the basic facts about the drug system need to be understood as well as possible.

The model described in this report has at least three distinct, but related, uses that can facilitate a more informed response to the marijuana trade. First, the model can be used to improve the estimation process. Many estimates are published in the public domain with little or no substantive explanation of how they are derived. Without a system framework, it is almost impossible to evaluate the accuracy of many basic estimates for the marijuana system. The model can be used to evaluate these estimates by examining their perturbation of the system and asking whether these perturbations are sensible. This technique can be especially effective if the analyst has relatively high certainty about some estimates, which can be used as "constraints" on the system. For example, an analyst can examine the INCSR and NNICC estimates of marijuana available for consumption in terms of the system implications for the number of users and compare it to the NIDA Household Survey estimate of the number of users to see if the production estimates make sense. Alternatively, the analyst can examine the plausibility of changes in other parameters (such as annual consumption) required to reconcile these estimates. Second, the model can be used to perform sensitivity analysis. Since there is a lot of uncertainty over many of the estimates, knowing which ones have the greatest impact on important outcomes in the United States can facilitate a more cost-efficient allocation of analytic resources. Third, the model can be used as a tool for more effective planning and assessment. It can help planners think in terms of a strategic framework, linking assumptions about production in Southeast Asia, for example, to marijuana flows in the United States.

Appendix

A. U.S. Region Definitions

The U.S. regions below are used by drug control agencies in tracking the movement and concentration of drugs. Table A.1 shows the regional compositions.

Table A.1

Regional Definitions

NORTHEAST	SOUTH CENTRAL	NORTH CENTRAL
Connecticut	Alabama	Colorado
Delaware	Arkansas	Idaho
Maine	Louisiana	Illinois
Massachusetts	Mississippi	Indiana
Maryland	Tennessee	Iowa
New Hampshire		Kansas
New Jersey	SOUTHWEST	Kentucky
New York	Arizona	Michigan
Pennsylvania	New Mexico	Minnesota
Rhode Island	Oklahoma	Missouri
Vermont	Texas	Montana
		Nebraska
SOUTHEAST	WEST	North Dakota
District of Columbia	California	Ohio
Florida	Nevada	South Dakota
Georgia	Oregon	Utah
North Carolina	Washington	Wisconsin
South Carolina		Wyoming
Puerto Rico		
Virgin Islands		
Virginia		
West Virginia		

B. For the User: More Detail About the Spreadsheet System

The Spreadsheets

A schematic of the spreadsheet organization is shown in Figure B.1 where the linkages are denoted by lines. Because the data are sparse, the database spreadsheets represented with shaded lines do not exist, but they are included in the figure for conceptual accuracy. The data contained in these spreadsheets come primarily from the *International Narcotics Control Strategy Report* (INCSR), the *National Narcotics Intelligence Consumers Committee Report* (NNICC), DEA reports, Congressional Hearings, and other publicly available sources. The production-related database contains data over several years, but the system spreadsheets model the quantities and flows of drug for one year at a time. After describing the spreadsheets in greater detail, this section provides some general guidelines for using the model.

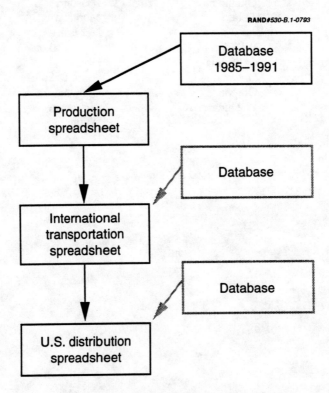

RAND#530-B.1-0793

Figure B.1—Spreadsheet Schematic

Database Spreadsheet

The first spreadsheet is the database and is the starting point for the model; it provides the initial conditions for the production spreadsheet. The user can also substitute his or her own data. This spreadsheet, schematically displayed in Figure B.2, includes a glossary of terms, the database, a "criteria" range and a "data extract" range, which is linked to the next spreadsheet.[1]

Each record in the database is a specific combination of country, year, source reference, and reference low or high value. Table B.1 shows a selection of observations. Column A contains the country, column B the year, and column C the source reference.[2] For each observation, over 25 data elements (fields) can be tracked. Table B.2 shows the list of data elements and their definitions reproduced from the glossary in the database spreadsheet.

The last two areas in the database spreadsheet are devoted to defining and extracting data from the database for use either in the system spreadsheets or for

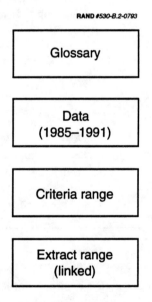

RAND #530-B.2-0793

Glossary

Data
(1985–1991)

Criteria range

Extract range
(linked)

Figure B.2—Database Spreadsheet Outline

---

[1]These are spreadsheet terms. The criteria range is where the user defines what data he or she wants to extract from the database; for instance, all observations for Mexico from 1985 to 1991. The extract range is where the subset of data defined in the criteria range are displayed.

[2]The source reference numbers are coded to specific reports identified on the spreadsheet. Sources that are used in a more limited way are included in the other spreadsheets as notes behind the relevant data cell(s).

32

Table B.1

Notional Observation Format

A	B	C
Country	Year	Reference
Mexico	1991	[2] Low
Mexico	1991	[2] High
Colombia	1991	[2] Low
Colombia	1991	[2] High
Jamaica	1991	[2] Low
Jamaica	1991	[2] High

NOTE: Bracketed figures [] refer to specific source, e.g., INCSR.

Table B.2

Cultivation and Conversion Factors: Marijuana

Glossary Variable Name	Units of Measure	Explanation
MARIJYIELDMT	metric tons/hectare	Amount of marijuana (in metric tons) per cultivated hectare
MARIJYIELDKg	Kg/hectare	Amount of marijuana (in kilograms) per cultivated hectare
CULTIVAREA	hectares	Cultivation area
ERADAREA	hectares	Eradication area
NETCULTIVAREA	hectares	Net cultivation area (after eradication)
MARIJHARVEST	metric tons	(Cultivation minus eradication) times yield
MARIJCONSUMD	metric tons	Marijuana consumed in country
MARIJSEIZD	metric tons	Marijuana seized in country
MARIJLOST	metric tons	Marijuana losses in country
NETMARIJ	metric tons	Marijuana harvest minus the three loss categories
MARIJEXPORTED	metric tons	Marijuana exported

summary statistics.[3] These areas are partially reproduced in Table B.3. The criteria range is where the user enters the desired characteristics of observations to be extracted. In our example, we have requested observations for 1991 and the low value for reference 2 (which is the INCSR, March 1992). Using the Excel data extract command places observations that meet the criteria into the data extract range. It is the extract range that is linked to the Production spreadsheet. This is the form of the criteria request that should be used if the user wants the extracted data to be used by the systems spreadsheets, although any combination of year

---

[3]A database can provide an analyst with summary statistics about the data. For instance, the DAVERAGE function can be used to find the average cultivation area for all the observations in the database.

Table B.3

Database Criteria and Extract Range

CRITERIA

COUNTRY	YEAR	REFERENCE	MARIJYIELDMT	MARIJYIELDKg	CULTIVAREA	ERADAREA	NETCULTIVAREA
	1991	[2] LOW					
			XXXX				

EXTRACT
RANGE

COUNTRY	YEAR	REFERENCE	MARIJYIELDMT	MARIJYIELDKg	CULTIVAREA	ERADAREA	NETCULTIVAREA
Belize	1991	[2]LOW	0.91	907.4	320	266	54
Colombia	1991	[2]LOW	0.83	825.0	2,000	0	2,000
Jamaica	1991	[2]LOW	0.67	674.7	1,783	833	950
Mexico	1991	[2]LOW	0.43	434.0	28,710	10,795	17,915

and reference may be used. Otherwise, if the user wants to use the database exclusively, many creative combinations of criteria can be applied.

Production Spreadsheet

The first system spreadsheet is the production spreadsheet. This spreadsheet begins with the cultivation of the necessary raw material and concludes with the amount of marijuana ready for export to various markets. Data are presented on

- hectares of marijuana cultivated
- productivity factors
- loss factors (including consumption, in-country seizures, and other losses).

The general procedure followed in this spreadsheet is to calculate the gross marijuana, and then subtract losses, seizures, and consumption.[4] Almost all data elements in this spreadsheet are linked to the previous Database spreadsheet. However, they can be easily overridden if alternative data are available.

Table B.4 is a representation of the spreadsheet for the initial calculation—harvested area. It begins with cultivated areas for the principal marijuana producers,[5] subtracts losses due either to eradication or other (e.g., fields left fallow), yielding the harvested area. Factors for marijuana yields per hectare then appear and the multiplication takes us to the second stage—marijuana. In this illustration of 1991 data, Mexico cultivated an estimated 28,710 hectares of

---

[4]The implicit assumption is that the losses are of in-country produced goods.

[5]Note that "Other" is not included, nor is the United States. Marijuana production for "Other" can be added into the system at the beginning of the International Transportation spreadsheet and U.S. production can be added at the beginning of the U.S. Distribution spreadsheet.

Table B.4

Production Spreadsheet: First Stage—Cultivation and Production

	CULTIVATED HECTARES BEFORE LOSSES	ERAD. AREA	OTHER LOSS	CULTIVATED HECTARES AFTER LOSSES	MARIJUANA YIELD FACTORS (Calculated)
BELIZE	320	266	0	54	0.91
COLOMBIA	2,000	0	0	2,000	0.83
JAMAICA	1,783	833	0	950	0.67
MEXICO	28,710	10,795	0	17,915	0.43
TOTAL	32,813	11,894	0	20,919	

marijuana in 1991; a large percentage, nearly 40 percent, was eradicated (10,795). On average, in 1991, 1 hectare yielded 430 kilograms (or 0.430 metric tons) of marijuana, yielding about 7,775 metric tons of marijuana available for transport to the world's markets, and looking to the next stage, we see that this is the amount with which Mexico begins.

As can be seen in Table B.5, Mexico has a calculated gross marijuana supply of 7,775 metric tons. At this point, losses from in-country consumption, seizures or other (e.g., spoilage, inventory shrinkage) are subtracted from gross marijuana yield. The estimated net marijuana (i.e., after losses) available for export to the world's markets is then linked to the next spreadsheet.

International Transportation

This spreadsheet begins with final product ready for export from the Production spreadsheet just described, and it estimates the amount that is successfully smuggled into the United States. Simply, as the schematic in Figure B.3 shows, it is a series of input matrices that systematically divides the drug volume from producer countries, to shipping countries, to markets, to U.S. regions, and finally to U.S. regions and transportation modes. This spreadsheet contains the following estimates

- the amount transiting each smuggler country
- the amount exported to markets other than the United States
- the amount coming into the United States
- the amount, net of seizures, that makes it into the United States by region and transportation mode.

Table B.5

Production Spreadsheet: Second Stage—Marijuana

(1) Marijuana BEFORE LOSSES AND TRANSFERS		Marijuana CONSUMED	Marijuana SEIZED	Marijuana OTHER LOSS	(2) Marijuana AFTER LOSSES
			—MINUS—		
BELIZE	49	10	8	2	29
COLOMBIA	1,650	2	329	0	1,319
JAMAICA	641	0	43	0	598
MEXICO	7,775	100	255	0	7,420
TOTAL	10,115	112	635	2	9,366

RAND#530-B.3-0793

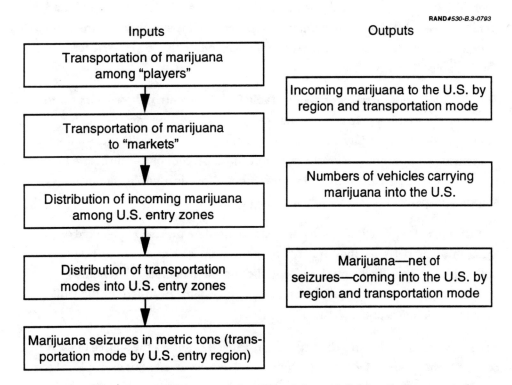

Inputs

- Transportation of marijuana among "players"
- Transportation of marijuana to "markets"
- Distribution of incoming marijuana among U.S. entry zones
- Distribution of transportation modes into U.S. entry zones
- Marijuana seizures in metric tons (transportation mode by U.S. entry region)

Outputs

- Incoming marijuana to the U.S. by region and transportation mode
- Numbers of vehicles carrying marijuana into the U.S.
- Marijuana—net of seizures—coming into the U.S. by region and transportation mode

Figure B.3—International Transportation Spreadsheet: A Schematic Representation

Table B.6 shows the amount of marijuana ready for export to the world's markets; an estimated 12,866 metric tons of marijuana are ready for export to the world's market. The database contains data for the four principal suppliers of marijuana to the United States. Additional countries were not included, because the data were not available (at least in the NNICC and INCSR reports). However, both the NNICC and the INCSR publish data for "other," even though it is not clear where this marijuana is grown. As a result, we have provided the

Table B.6

Estimate of Marijuana Ready for the World's Markets

	"MARIPROD" (in metric tons) (1)	Marijuana FROM INVENTORY/ STORAGE (2)	ALTERNATIVE INPUTS (3)
BELIZE	29	0.0	#N/A
COLOMBIA	1,319	0.0	#N/A
JAMAICA	598	0.0	#N/A
MEXICO	7,420	0.0	#N/A
"Other"	3,500	0.0	#N/A
Country 2	0	0.0	#N/A
TOTAL	12,866	0.0	#N/A

user with the option to type in the name of any source—be it "other," Thailand, Brazil, etc.—and the estimated amount of marijuana it is supplying to the United States. For 1991, the estimated production from "other" is 3,500 metric tons, and this is depicted in Table B.6.[6]

The transshipment matrix is shown in Table B.7. This matrix allows the user to transship the marijuana to other countries.[7] In this case, one can see that 50 percent of Belize's marijuana and 25 percent of Colombia's marijuana is shipped to Mexico. Also, Colombia is estimated to ship 25 percent of its marijuana to the Bahamas and 25 percent to the Dominican Republic. Meanwhile, Jamaica is shipping 50 percent of its marijuana to the Bahamas.

Obviously, these percentages are not meant to imply a precise knowledge of these shipping patterns; they are only rough estimates. Nevertheless, they are not arbitrary. Both the Dominican Republic and the Bahamas are generally believed to be major transshipment points for marijuana destined for the United States from Jamaica and Colombia.

The source distribution matrix, depicted in Table B.8, shows the source of each country's marijuana after the transshipments have occurred. For example, of the marijuana currently held by Belize, 100 percent of it was grown in Belize. However, of the marijuana held by the Bahamas, 52.4 percent was grown in Colombia and 47.6 percent was grown in Jamaica.

---

[6]Also, all other relevant cells in the spreadsheet are linked to this cell, so it is only necessary to type in the source one time. There are also two "wildcard" cells, labeled Country 1 and Country 2. In the example shown in Table B.6, "other" has been substituted for Country 1.

[7]The model allows the user to type in up to three additional transshipment countries. These cells are otherwise labeled Country 3, Country 4, and Country 5.

Table B.7
Transshipment Matrix

(INPUT IN PERCENTS, CONVERTED TO METRIC TONS)
TRANSPORT TO:

FROM:	BELIZE	COLOMBIA	JAMAICA	MEXICO	Other	Country 2	The Bahama	Domin. Rep	Country 5	AMOUNT EXPORTED	AMOUNT IMPORTED	AMOUNT REMAINING
BELIZE	0%	0%	0%	50%	0%	0%	0%	0%	0%	50%		
29.0	0.0	0.0	0.0	14.5	0.0	0.0	0.0	0.0	0.0	14.5	0.0	14.5
COLOMBIA	0%		0%	25%	0%	0%	25%	25%	0%	75%		
1319.0	0.0		0.0	329.8	0.0	0.0	329.8	329.8	0.0	989.3	0.0	329.8
JAMAICA	0%	0%		0%	0%	0%	50%	0%	0%	50%		
598.0	0.0	0.0		0.0	0.0	0.0	299.0	0.0	0.0	299.0	0.0	299.0
MEXICO	0%	0%	0%		0%	0%	0%	0%	0%	0%		
7420.0	0.0	0.0	0.0		0.0	0.0	0.0	0.0	0.0	0.0	344.3	7764.3
Other	0%	0%	0%	0%		0%	0%	0%	0%	0%		
3500.0	0.0	0.0	0.0	0.0		0.0	0.0	0.0	0.0	0.0	0.0	3500.0
Country 2	0%	0%	0%	0%	0%		0%	0%	0%	0%		
0.0	0.0	0.0	0.0	0.0	0.0		0.0	0.0	0.0	0.0	0.0	0.0
AMOUNT IMPORTED	0.0	0.0	0.0	344.3	0.0	0.0	628.8	329.8	0.0	1302.8	344.3	11907.5

SUM CHECK:

Table B.8

Source Distribution (in percent)

	Belize	Colombia	Jamaica	Mexico	Other	Country 2	Total
Belize	100.0	0.0	0.0	0.0	0.0	0.0	100.0
Colombia	0.0	100.0	0.0	0.0	0.0	0.0	100.0
Jamaica	0.0	0.0	100.0	0.0	0.0	0.0	100.0
Mexico	0.2	4.2	0.0	95.6	0.0	0.0	100.0
Other	0.0	0.0	0.0	0.0	100.0	0.0	100.0
Country 2	0.0	0.0	0.0	0.0	0.0	0.0	0.0
The Bahamas	0.0	52.4	47.6	0.0	0.0	0.0	100.0
Domin. Rep.	0.0	100.0	0.0	0.0	0.0	0.0	100.0
Country 5	0.0	0.0	0.0	0.0	0.0	0.0	0.0

After the transshipments have occurred, the next matrix (Table 2 in the International Transportation spreadsheet) distributes the drug to the markets. Table B.9 is a representation of this matrix—sample shipping countries are listed in the left-hand column, and the markets are identified across the top row. The United States and Canada are identified separately, all other markets are denoted by continent. We have included an additional "market"—storage—which can hold the product for distribution in a later year.[8] Below each shipping country listed in the left-hand column is a figure representing the metric tons of marijuana ready for shipment to market. The user enters the percentage of this amount that is distributed to each market, and the computer calculates the metric tonnage right below the input value. For example, according to our calculations for 1991, Mexico had 7,764.3 metric tons of marijuana to smuggle, of which 75 percent was shipped to the United States.[9] On the other hand, 100 percent of "other" is shipped to the United States. The source or rationale for the 100-percent estimate is included in a note "behind" the cell and, in this example, is an estimate based on the DEA smuggling routes map (1989), the INCSR (1992), and other miscellaneous information[10] We have assumed that 75 percent of the marijuana grown in the four countries ultimately finds its way into the United States. Alternatively, the user can simply input the estimated percentage headed for the U.S. market and ignore the other markets. In either case, this matrix estimates the volume of drug being sent to the United States. The

---

[8]For simplicity, we have provided one storage point; conceptually there could be storage at most stages of the production process.

[9]The source distribution table indicates that, of Mexico's 7,764.3 metric tons of marijuana, 7,423 originated in Mexico, 326 metric tons were grown in Colombia, and 16 metric tons was cultivated in Belize.

[10]The existence of a note behind a cell is indicated by a small square (arrow on the Macintosh) in the upper right hand corner of the cell.

Table B.9

Illustrative Example: Shipping Marijuana to the World's Markets

FROM:	CANADA	S.E. ASIA/ PACIFIC	EUROPE/ MID.EAST	TO STORAGE	TO OTHER MARKETS	AMOUNT TO U.S.	ALT. AMOUNT TO U.S.
MEXICO	10.0%	0.0%	10.0%	5.0%	25%	75%	#N/A
7764.3	776.4	0.0	776.4	388.2	1,941.1	5,823.2	#N/A
"Other"	0.0%	0.0%	0.0%	0.0%	0%	100%	#N/A
0.0	0.0	0.0	0.0	0.0	0.0	3,500	#N/A

next step is to estimate how much is being smuggled into each region of the United States.

In the next table, the user must provide an estimate of the total amount of marijuana seized in foreign locations that was destined for the U.S. market. In this illustrative example, about 8.11 metric tons were seized in foreign locations (normally foreign ports) that were deemed to be destined for the United States. Since it is not known where this marijuana originated from (at least not to RAND), a proportional amount is subtracted from each country's total to remove this amount from the system (see Table B.10). So, if 0.08 percent of the total marijuana destined for the United States is seized in foreign locations, 0.08 percent of the marijuana is subtracted from each country that is shipping to the United States.

The next input matrix (not shown) is patterned very similarly to the one for distributing the marijuana to the world's markets, except in this case the marijuana is distributed to the six U.S. regions. The smuggling countries are shown in the left-hand column with the amount destined for the U.S. market, and the regions of the United States are shown across the top row (these regions are defined in Appendix A). The user enters the percentage smuggled from each

Table B.10

Foreign Seizures

10,524.5	estimated metric tons headed for the U.S. market BEFORE foreign seizures.
8.11	estimated metric tons destined for the United States but seized in foreign locations.
0.08%	of the total that is destined for the United States is seized in foreign locations.
10,516.4	estimated metric tons headed for the U.S. market AFTER foreign seizures.

shipping country to each region of the United States. The routes identified in this spreadsheet were approximated from a DEA map of drug trafficking routes. The absence of an entry indicates that there is no route between the shipping country and the U.S. region.[11]

The next input matrix is again patterned similarly to the previous two matrices (see Table B.11). It distributes the drug flow into each U.S. region among a number of transportation modes:

- Commercial air
- Private air
- Commercial sea
- Private sea
- Commercial land
- Private land.

Commercial air includes passengers carrying illicit drugs, as well as packaged drugs contained in cargo. Commercial land includes tractor trailers, while private land includes private and recreational vehicles, as well as persons carrying packages. The others are self-explanatory. The distribution of drug traffic into these transportation modes can be based on seizure or other relevant data. For convenience, illustrative default distributions are provided. The distributions are specific to each entry region; that is, every route feeding the Southeast United States will have the same distribution based on the seizures in that region. (Default values can be easily overridden.)

The final input matrix in the International Transportation spreadsheet is for estimates of seizures, roughly limited to those at U.S. borders (see Table B.12).

Within the International Transportation spreadsheet, and several columns to the right of these input matrices, are tables of results. The first table shows the amounts of the drug smuggled over the various routes to the United States.

Table B.11

Marijuana Entering U.S. Regions by Transportation Mode (in percent)

	North-Central	North-east	South-east	South-Central	South-west	West
Commercial air	100	45	11	8	0	1
Private air	0	0	11	0	1	0
Commercial land	0	0	XXX	XXX	17	1
Private land	0	0	XXX	XXX	77	45
Commercial sea	0	54	11	16	1	12
Private sea	0	1	67	75	4	40
Total	100	100	100	100	100	100

---

[11]Drug Trafficking Routes, DEA Map, 1989.

Table B.12

Marijuana Seizures by Region and Transportation Mode

	North-Central	North-east	South-east	South-Central	South-west	West	Total by Mode
Commercial air	0.411	6.146	4.478	0.411	0.411	0.411	12.3
Private air	0.000	0.000	4.502	0.000	0.949	0.000	5.5
Commercial land	0.000	0.000	XXX	XXX	16.015	0.222	16.2
Private land	0.000	0.000	XXX	XXX	72.840	13.040	85.9
Commercial sea	0.000	7.324	4.514	0.809	0.809	3.577	17.0
Private sea	0.000	0.205	26.859	3.692	3.692	11.625	46.1
Total by region	0.4	13.7	40.4	4.9	94.7	28.9	182.9

Table B.13 shows a section of this table. Each entry in the table represents the estimate of metric tonnage of marijuana that traveled from the shipping countries listed in the left-hand column to the U.S. entry region listed along the top row, sorted by transportation mode. For example, an estimated 41.41 metric tons traveled from Mexico to the West region of the United States by commercial air in 1991.

The same format is repeated for the other transportation modes, and this information, coupled with data on average load sizes, can be used to estimate the number of land, sea, and air vehicles carrying the marijuana into the United States. Finally, various summary statistics are offered, and Table B.14 shows some of them.

The analyst can view the consequences and implications of his or her parameters and estimates up to this point in the model. For example, 45.5 percent of all marijuana enters through the West region, followed by 31 percent in the Southwest. Planners should ask themselves whether this conforms to current planning and assumptions. If not, can the differences be understood or

Table B.13

Output: Volume of Marijuana by Route and Transportation Mode

Commercial Air	North-Central	North-east	South-east	South-Central	South-west	West	Totals
Belize	0.0	0.0	0.72	0.36	0.0	0.0	1.09
Colombia	0.0	0.0	13.71	0.0	0.0	1.76	15.47
Jamaica	0.0	10.07	19.89	1.87	0.0	0.0	31.84
Mexico	0.0	0.0	0.0	0.0	12.62	41.41	54.04
Other	349.73	157.18	38.81	29.26	1.52	24.89	601.39
Country 2	0.0	0.0	0.0	0.0	0.0	0.0	0.0
The Bahamas	0.0	0.0	31.37	15.77	0.0	0.0	47.14
Domin. Rep.	0.0	0.0	16.45	8.27	0.0	0.0	24.72
Country 5	0.0	0.0	0.0	0.0	0.0	0.0	0.0

Table B.14

Summary Statistics for Marijuana Entering the United States

BY REGION:	North-Central	North-East	South-East	South-Central	South-West	West
	349.7	372.1	1,090.1	663.8	3,259.1	4,781.6
TOTALS	3.3%	3.5%	10.4%	6.3%	31.0%	45.5%

TOTALS BY TRANSPORT MODE:		
AIR:	930.0	8.8%
commercial	775.7	7.4%
private	154.3	1.5%
LAND:	5,253.5	50.0%
commercial	587.8	5.6%
private	4,665.7	44.4%
SEA:	4,332.9	41.2%
commercial	1,050.7	10.0%
private	3,282.2	31.2%

TOTALS BY EXPORT COUNTRY		
Belize	10.9	0.1%
Colombia	247.1	2.3%
Jamaica	224.1	2.1%
Mexico	5818.7	55.3%
Other	3497.3	33.3%
Country 2	0.0	0.0%
Bahamas	471.2	4.5%
Domin. Rep.	247.1	2.3%
Country 5	0.0	0.0%

TOTALS BY SOURCE COUNTRY		
Belize	21.7	0.2%
Colombia	988.5	9.4%
Jamaica	448.2	4.3%
Mexico	5,560.7	52.9%
Other	3,497.3	33.3%
Country 2	0.0	0.0%
	10,516.4	100%

reconciled? Also, regarding the issue of totals by source country, does the percentage distribution among the countries conform to the distributions reported in the annual NNICC reports?

U.S. Distribution

The final system spreadsheet tracks the domestic distribution of marijuana. It begins with the amount successfully smuggled into each of the U.S. entry regions. (Again, while these values are linked to the previous spreadsheet, they can be overridden.) A column is available to add domestic production to the amount imported. This table generates an estimate of the total amount of marijuana available for domestic distribution.

The remainder of this spreadsheet distributes the drug throughout the United States and calculates the numbers of individuals in each of the drug-market hierarchy levels, based on estimates of the supply and annual use. The final table compares the estimated user-prevalence rates with the National Institute of Drug

Abuse (NIDA) National Household Survey estimate.[12] Even fewer data are available for this part of the system description than for the production and international transportation sections, so almost all the numbers shown here are meant to be illustrative.

Figure B.4 shows a schematic of this spreadsheet. Once we have the estimate of the amount of drug entering the various U.S. regions, we provide the capability to estimate interregional transfers (e.g., from the Northeast to the South-Central United States).

Table B.15 shows the estimated marijuana entering the various regions of the United States, and the estimated domestic production by region. The estimate presented here is based on the assumption that 5,000 to 6,000 metric tons are produced and that this marijuana is primarily grown in states within these four regions.[13]

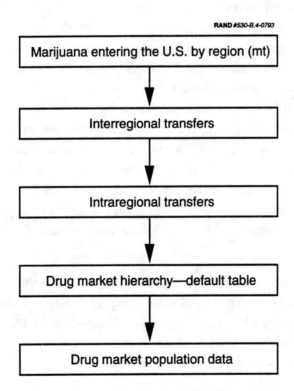

RAND #530-B.4-0793

Figure B.4—U.S. Distribution Spreadsheet: A Schematic Representation

---

[12]National Household Survey on Drug Abuse: Population Estimates 1988, U.S. Department of Health and Human Services, National Institute on Drug Abuse, 1989.

[13]The 1990 NNICC report provides this information. It indicates that the five major cultivated cannabis-producing states in 1990 were Missouri, Oklahoma, Nebraska, Hawaii, and Kentucky (p. 31).

Table B.15

Incoming Marijuana by Region

	Net of POE Seizures	Domestic Production	Total	Alternate Total
North-Central	349.3	1,400	1,749.3	#N/A
Northeast	358.5	0	358.5	#N/A
Southeast	1,049.7	0	1,049.7	#N/A
South-Central	658.9	1,400	2,058.9	#N/A
Southwest	3,164.4	1,400	4,564.4	#N/A
West	4,752.7	1,400	6,152.7	#N/A
Total	10,333.6	5,600	15,933.5	#N/A

The procedure here mirrors the procedure in the International Transportation spreadsheet. The user enters the estimate of the percentage of the total drug available that is shipped from the entry regions to the demand regions, then enters estimates of the losses due either to domestic enforcement or to inventory or other losses. The user then has the option to allocate the regional quantities to cities within the region. The cities included are those identified as high-intensity trafficking areas by the National Drug Control Strategy Report, January 1990, augmented by those classified by the FBI as Level I or II cities for drug trafficking activities. The next two matrices contain inputs for the final table, which in turn calculates the numbers of individuals involved in the trade at each level in the market. The regions and cities appear in the left-hand column, and the trade hierarchy appears across the top. Each entry represents the number of individuals involved in the trade for the given year based on the drug supply. The final columns compare the drug user prevalence (based on supply estimates) to a demand-based estimate of drug use to determine whether the two estimates are at all consistent.

This final table is reproduced in Table B.16, and as one can see, the estimated number of marijuana users is several times higher than the estimate provided by NIDA from the National Household Survey on Drug Abuse.[14] This result can be used to go back into the model and to question whether some production or distribution estimates are reasonable.

Summary Spreadsheet

There is one final spreadsheet, the Summary Spreadsheet. This spreadsheet does not require any data input by the user, and the only new information is the

---

[14]One should not interpret this as our definitive estimate of the number of marijuana users in the United States. Rather, it should be interpreted as the number of users there must be *if one accepts all previous parameter estimates in the model.*

Table B.16

Drug Market Population Data

	Estimated Users (in 000s)	Population (in 000s)	Calculated Prevalence	National Household Survey Prevalence	Ratio
North Central					
Chicago (II)	0	0	NA	9.2%	NA
Detroit (II)	0	0	NA	9.2%	NA
All other	14,294	58,031	24.6%	9.2%	2.62
Northeast					
Boston (II)	0	0	NA	10.0%	NA
Newark (II)	0	0	NA	10.0%	NA
New York (I)	0	0	NA	10.0%	NA
All other	2,894	47,152	6.1%	9.9%	0.62
Southeast					
Atlanta	0	0	NA	8.6%	NA
Miami (I)	0	0	NA	8.6%	NA
All other	8,560	30,996	27.6%	8.6%	3.21
South Central					
New Orleans	0	0	NA	8.6%	NA
All other	16,832	14,860	113.3%	8.6%	13.17
Southwest					
El Paso (~I)	0	0	NA	8.6%	NA
Houston (I)	0	0	NA	8.6%	NA
All other	37,369	19,900	187.8%	9.2%	20.36
West					
Los Angeles (I)	0	0	NA	11.7%	NA
San Diego (II)	0	0	NA	11.7%	NA
San Francisco (II)	0	0	NA	11.7%	NA
Seattle	0	0	NA	11.7%	NA
All other	50,388	30,193	166.9%	11.7%	14.26
U.S. total	130,337	201,132	64.8%	9.6%	

percentage distribution to the world's markets. This is obtained by combining information on consumption within the producing countries with marijuana shipments to the world's markets. In short, for the sake of convenience, this spreadsheet pulls together selected information from the other spreadsheets (see Figure B.5).

	Year	1991	
Marijuana Ready for Export to the World Market		9,366	metric tons
Percentage Distribution to the World Markets			
Canada		6.5%	
SEA/Pacific		0.0%	
Europe/Middle East		8.0%	
Storage		3.6%	
United States		81.8%	
Amount of Marijuana Entering the United States		15,933.5	metric tons
Source Distribution of Marijuana		Foreign	Total
Belize		0.2%	0.1%
Colombia		9.4%	6.1%
Jamaica		4.3%	2.8%
Mexico		52.9%	34.3%
Other		33.3%	21.6%
Country 2		0.0%	0.0%
United States		n.a.	35.1%
Estimated Number of Users in the United States		130,336,631	

Figure B.5—The Summary Spreadsheet

C. Spreadsheet Guidelines

The system description consists of four spreadsheets:

1. MARIDATA for the marijuana database

2. MARIPROD for processing and movement

3. MARITRAN for international transportation

4. MARIUSA for U.S. distribution.

The graphs associated with the worksheets are saved in separate files known as chart files.

Each spreadsheet has cells that are linked to data in the previous worksheet, so all the spreadsheets must be open. The chart files should generally be open as well. Any spreadsheets not of immediate interest can be hidden with the **Window Hide** command. Once the worksheets are all open, they can be saved with the **File Save Workspace** command. A workspace file contains a list of all the documents open at the time you choose the **Save Workspace** command. So the next time you use the model, you can open the files all at once just by clicking on the workspace file.

A spreadsheet that has cells linked to data in another worksheet is called "dependent" on that other worksheet. For instance, MARIPROD is dependent on MARIDATA; MARITRAN is dependent on MARIPROD; and so on. As long as all the dependent worksheets are open, if you save a worksheet under a different name, the linked cell references in the dependent worksheet(s) will also change. If a chart file is open (and not hidden), any changes made in the data it is linked to will be immediately reflected in the graph.

Linked cells use absolute addresses (not relative addresses for the cells they link to). So, let us say you expanded the database in MARIDATA, and your data extract range now starts at row 230 rather than row 226. You will get incorrect (if any) data in the linked dependent cells in MARIPROD unless you manually change the address those cells link to. (See the Excel manual.) You will also need to redefine the database range in MARIDATA using the **Data Set Database** command.

It is good practice to make a working copy of the original "master" files and store the master files in a safe place—perhaps a separate directory (PC) or folder

(Mac). It is also good practice to click on the *Read Only* option in the Open Document dialog box. When this box is checked, the program allows you to view and edit the file, but requires you to save it under another name so you cannot overwrite the file you started with. This feature is especially helpful if you are doing, say, sensitivity analyses and want to save several versions with different data estimates.

Nomenclature

Blue cells are meant to alert the user that they are linked to other worksheets. Of course, the user may override and enter other data, but to restore these links they will have to use the "master" version (or a knowledgeable user can restore them manually). Red cells indicate a user should enter his or her own data.

Other cells with a little red square (IBM) or arrow (Apple) in the upper right-hand corner have a note "behind" the cell explaining something about the data in the cell, or if there is a column of like numbers the note may reference the entire column (in a column of numbers it may only be the first cell that has a note). This note can be viewed by using the command **Formula Note** or by double-clicking on the cell. The dialog box will also show a list of other notes in the spreadsheet that can be viewed by clicking on any entry in the list. See the Excel manual about viewing or printing all the notes on a spreadsheet.

Some Features of Using the Database in MARIDATA

Users who are unfamiliar with using a spreadsheet database are strongly encouraged to read the Excel manual chapter on analyzing and reporting database information.

The defined criteria range in the master spreadsheet has two rows under the field names. Excel treats criteria entered on the same row as a logical "and", while criteria entered on difference rows are treated as a logical "or". In the example in the main text, "1989" is entered under the field name "YEAR" and "[2]LOW" is entered in the same row under the field named "REFERENCE." In extracting records, the program interprets this to mean, pick those records that have a year of 1989 *and* a reference of [2]LOW. If no criterion is entered under a field name, the program interprets it to mean, pick any (all) criteria for that field. Thus, if an entire row in the criteria range is left completely blank, the program will extract all records in the database. It is good practice to put stoppers in the form of "XXXX" or the like under a field name in each row in the criteria range to avoid inadvertently extracting all the data records.

In the master spreadsheet, the extract range is at the bottom of the spreadsheet and is defined as the row of field names. This is done to avoid guessing at how much space might be needed to extract records. However, each time you use the **Data Extract** command, all previous data in the extract range are cleared. If you want to save these data for some reason, copy them to another area of the worksheet or to another worksheet. A database can provide an analyst with summary statistics about the data. For instance, the DAVERAGE function can be used to find the average cultivation area. See Database Functions in the Excel manual.

Cell Locations

The figures on the following pages depict the various sections of the four spreadsheets. The text across from each figure describes that section of the spreadsheet.

	A	B	C	D	E	F	G	H	I	J	K
1	LINKED TO MARIDATA									PAGE 1	
2	ALLOWS USER INPUT				PROCESSING AND MOVEMENT: Marijuana						
3					YEAR=	1991					
4	CULTIVATION/PRODUCTION										
5	(In Hectares)										
6											
7	(1)				--MINUS--		(2)				
8	CULTIVATED HECTARES				ERAD.	OTHER	CULTIVATED HECTARES			LEAF YIELD	
9	BEFORE LOSSES				AREA	LOSS	AFTER LOSSES			FACTORS	
10											
11	Belize		320		266	0	54			0.91	
12	Colombia		2,000		0	0	2,000			0.83	
13	Jamaica		1,783		833	0	950			0.67	
14	Mexico		28,710		10,795	0	17,915			0.43	
15			TOTAL				TOTAL				
16			32,813				20,919				
17					Note: ERAD. AREA Linked to MARIDATA;						
18					OTHER LOSS not linked.						
19											
20	SECOND STAGE -- MARIJUANA										
21	(In Metric Tons)										
22											
23	(1)				-- MINUS--		(2)				
24	MARIJ BEFORE LOSSES				MARIJ	MARIJ	MARIJ		MARIJ AFTER		
25	AND TRANSFERS				CONSUMED	SEIZED	OTHERLOSS		LOSSES		
26											
27	Belize		49		10	8	2		29		
28	Colombia		1,650		2	329	0		1,319		
29	Jamaica		641		0	43	0		598		
30	Mexico		7,775		100	255	0		7,420		
31		TOTAL							TOTAL		
32			10,115						9,366		
33											

Figure C.1—The Marijuana Production Spreadsheet (cells A1 to K33)

Figure C.1 shows all of pertinent tables within MARIPROD.XLS. For example, the number of Mexico's cultivated hectares before losses (28,710) is shown in cell C14, eradication area (10,795) in cell E14, and other losses (0) in cell F14. The number for estimated hectares after losses (17,915) is shown in G14. The estimated leaf yield factor, or the metric tons of marijuana produced from one hectare (0.43), is displayed in cell J14. Since Mexico has an estimated 17,915 hectares and a leaf yield factor of 0.43, the resulting estimated production of marijuana is 7,775 metric tons, which is illustrated in cell C30. Mexican consumption (100), seizures (255), and other losses (0) are presented in cells E30, F30, and G30, respectively. The resulting estimate of Mexican marijuana production ready for export to the world's markets (7,420) is shown in cell I30.

SCREEN 1

INTERNATIONAL TRANSPORTATION: MARIJUANA

YEAR = 1991

Marijuana from MARIPROD.XLS (IN MTs)	INVENTORY (1)	FROM STORAGE (2)	ALTERNATIVE INPUTS (3)
Belize	29	0.0	#N/A
Colombia	1,319	0.0	#N/A
Jamaica	598	0.0	#N/A
Mexico	7,420	0.0	#N/A
Other	3500.0	0.0	#N/A
Country 2	0.0	0.0	#N/A
TOTAL	12,866	TOTAL 0.0	TOTAL #N/A

NOTE:
TABLE 1. USES COL. (1) DATA LINKED TO MARIPROD.XLS
PLUS COL.(2) DATA INPUT BY USER-
UNLESS ANY ALTERNATIVE DATA IS ENTERED IN COL. (3).
COL. (2) INPUTS SHOULD BE STORAGE FROM PRIOR YEAR(S).

TABLE 1. TRANSPORTATION OF MARIJUANA AMONG THE "PLAYERS"
(INPUT IN PERCENTS, CONVERTED TO METRIC TONS)

TRANSPORT TO:

FROM:	BELIZE	COLOMBIA	JAMAICA	MEXICO	Other	Country 2	The Bahama	Domin. Rep	Country 5	AMOUNT EXPORTED	AMOUNT IMPORTED	AMOUNT REMAINING
BELIZE		0%	0%	50%	0%	0%	0%	0%	0%	50%		
29.0		0.0	0.0	14.5	0.0	0.0	0.0	0.0	0.0	14.5	0.0	14.5
COLOMBIA	0%		0%	25%	0%	0%	25%	25%	0%	75%		
1319.0	0.0		0.0	329.8	0.0	0.0	329.8	329.8	0.0	989.3	0.0	329.8
JAMAICA	0%	0%		0%	0%	0%	50%	0%	0%	50%		
598.0	0.0	0.0		0.0	0.0	0.0	299.0	0.0	0.0	299.0	0.0	299.0
MEXICO	0%	0%	0%		0%	0%	0%	0%	0%	0%		
7420.0	0.0	0.0	0.0		0.0	0.0	0.0	0.0	0.0	0.0	344.3	7764.3
Other	0%	0%	0%	0%		0%	0%	0%	0%	0%		
3500.0	0.0	0.0	0.0	0.0		0.0	0.0	0.0	0.0	0.0	0.0	3500.0
Country 2	0%	0%	0%	0%	0%		0%	0%	0%	0%		
0.0	0.0	0.0	0.0	0.0	0.0		0.0	0.0	0.0	0.0	0.0	0.0
AMOUNT IMPORTED	0.0	0.0	0.0	344.3	0.0	0.0	628.8	329.8	0.0	1302.8	344.3	11907.5

SOURCE DISTRIBUTION

	Belize	Colombia	Jamaica	Mexico	Other	Country 2	SUM
Belize	100.0%	0.0%	0.0%	0.0%	0.0%	0.0%	100%
Colombia	0.0%	100.0%	0.0%	0.0%	0.0%	0.0%	100%
Jamaica	0.0%	0.0%	100.0%	0.0%	0.0%	0.0%	100%
Mexico	0.2%	4.2%	0.0%	95.6%	0.0%	0.0%	100%
Other	0.0%	0.0%	0.0%	0.0%	100.0%	0.0%	100%
Country 2	0.0%	0.0%	0.0%	0.0%	0.0%	0.0%	0%
The Bahamas	0.0%	52.4%	47.6%	0.0%	0.0%	0.0%	100%
Domin. Rep.	0.0%	100.0%	0.0%	0.0%	0.0%	0.0%	100%
Country 5	0.0%	0.0%	0.0%	0.0%	0.0%	0.0%	0%

SUM CHECKS

Figure C.2—Transporting Marijuana Among the "Players" (cells A1 to AI45)

Figure C.2 shows the first section of the marijuana transportation spreadsheet, MARITRAN.XLS. The user may decide whether to ship marijuana from one country to another. Mexico's estimated marijuana production ready for export (7,420) is presented in cell C12. This value is then carried down to cell A34. None of Mexico's marijuana is transported to other countries, but Mexico receives some marijuana. Belize, for instance, is shipping 50 percent of its marijuana to Mexico. This is indicated in cell I24. Moreover, Colombia is shipping 25 percent of its marijuana to Mexico, as indicated in cell I27. After the user inputs the relevant percentages, formulas will automatically calculate the appropriate amount of marijuana. Mexico ends up with 7,764.3 metric tons of marijuana, as revealed in cell Y34. Also, one can see in cell AC38 that 0.2 percent of the marijuana in Mexico was grown in Belize; 4.2 percent was produced Colombia; and 95.6 percent was grown in Mexico. (Note: The user can input new countries into cells A13, A14, O22, Q22, or S22. These countries will appear in the appropriate spreadsheet locations throughout the rest of the spreadsheet. This feature is useful if different countries from those otherwise displayed in the model begin to play a more prominent role in the marijuana system.)

	A	B	C	D	E	F	G	H	I	J	K	L	M	N	O	P
46																
47																
48																
49																
50	TABLE 2: TRANSPORTATION OF MARIJUANA TO "MARKETS" (COUNTRIES/CONTINENTS)															
51					(INPUT IN PERCENTS, CONVERTED TO METRIC TONS)											
52							TRANSPORT TO:				SUBTOTAL				ALTERNATIVE	
53							S.E.ASIA/		EUROPE/		TO		TO OTHER		AMOUNT		AMOUNT
54	FROM:		CANADA		PACIFIC		MID.EAST		STORAGE		MARKETS		TO U.S.		TO U.S.
55			-------------		-------------		-------------		-------------		-------------		-------------		-------------
56	BELIZE		0%		0%		20%		5%		25%		75%		#N/A
57	14.5		0.0		0.0		2.9		0.7		3.6		10.9		#N/A
58			-------------		-------------		-------------		-------------		-------------		-------------		-------------
59	COLOMBIA		10%		0%		10%		5%		25%		75%		#N/A
60	329.8		33.0		0.0		33.0		16.5		82.4		247.3		#N/A
61			-------------		-------------		-------------		-------------		-------------		-------------		-------------
62	JAMAICA		10%		0%		10%		5%		25%		75%		#N/A
63	299.0		29.9		0.0		29.9		15.0		74.8		224.3		#N/A
64			-------------		-------------		-------------		-------------		-------------		-------------		-------------
65	MEXICO		10%		0%		10%		5%		25%		75%		#N/A
66	7764.3		776.4		0.0		776.4		388.2		1941.1		5823.2		#N/A
67			-------------		-------------		-------------		-------------		-------------		-------------		-------------
68	Other		0%		0%		0%		0%		0%		100%		#N/A
69	3500.0		0.0		0.0		0.0		0.0		0.0		3500.0		#N/A
70			-------------		-------------		-------------		-------------		-------------		-------------		-------------
71	Country 2		0%		0%		0%		0%		0%		0%		#N/A
72	0.0		0.0		0.0		0.0		0.0		0.0		0.0		#N/A
73			-------------		-------------		-------------		-------------		-------------		-------------		-------------
74	The Baham		0%		0%		20%		5%		25%		75%		#N/A
75	628.8		0.0		0.0		125.8		31.4		157.2		471.6		#N/A
76			-------------		-------------		-------------		-------------		-------------		-------------		-------------
77	Domin. Rep		0%		0%		20%		5%		25%		75%		#N/A
78	329.8		0.0		0.0		66.0		16.5		82.4		247.3		#N/A
79			-------------		-------------		-------------		-------------		-------------		-------------		-------------
80	Country 5		0%		0%		0%		0%		0%		0%		#N/A
81	0.0		0.0		0.0		0.0		0.0		0.0		0.0		#N/A
82			-------------		-------------		-------------		-------------		-------------		-------------		-------------
83	TOTALS		839.3		0.0		1033.9		468.3		2341.5		10524.5		#N/A
84			Canada	S.E. Asia/Pac.			Eur/M.E.		Storage		Total Other		U.S.			
85			6.5%		0.0%		8.0%		3.6%		18.2%		81.8%			
86	TABLE 3: FOREIGN SEIZURES															
87	10524.5	estimated Metric Tons headed for the U.S. market BEFORE foreign seizure														
88	8.11	estimated Metric Tons destined for the U.S. but seized in foreign locations														
89	0.08%	of the total that is destined for U.S. but is seized in foreign locations.														
90	10516.4	estimated Metric Tons headed for the U.S. market AFTER foreign seizures.														
91																

Figure C.3—Transportation of Marijuana to "Markets" and Foreign Seizures (cells A46 to P91)

Figure C.3 shows the next section of the marijuana transportation spreadsheet, MARITRAN.XLS. The user may decide on which markets to send a country's marijuana. Mexico's estimated marijuana production ready for shipment to the world's markets (7,764.3) is presented in cell A66. This marijuana can be allocated to the world's markets by placing a percentage in cells C65 for Canada, E65 for Southeast Asia and the Pacific, G65 for Europe and the Middle East, I65 for storage, and M65 for the United States. One can see, for example, that 75 percent of Mexico's marijuana is shipped to the United States, as indicated in cell M65. The total amount of marijuana shipped to the United States (10,524.5) by all countries is presented in cell M83, which represents 81.8 percent of all marijuana shipped to market (cell M85). (Note: The user can also provide alternative amounts to the United States in column O and ignore the amounts going to other markets.) The estimate of 10,524.5 metric tons is carried down to cell A87. The user must then provide an estimate of how much marijuana destined for the United States is seized in *foreign locations* (8.11), as shown in cell A88. This amount is subtracted from the system, and the resulting net amount remaining (10,516.4) is provided in cell A90.

	A	B	C	D	E	F	G	H	I	J	K	L	M	N	O	P	Q	R
92																		
93	TABLE 4: DISTRIBUTION OF INCOMING MARIJUANA AMONG U.S. ENTRY REGIONS																	
94					(INPUT IN PERCENTS, CONVERTED TO METRIC TONS)													
95					TRANSPORT TO:													
96			NORTH-		NORTH-		SOUTH-		SOUTH-		SOUTH-				AMOUNT			
97	FROM:		CENTRAL		EAST		EAST		CENTRAL		WEST		WEST		REMAINING		CHECKSUM	
98			---------------		---------------		---------------		---------------		---------------		---------------		---------------		---------------	
99	BELIZE		0%		0%		60%		40%		0%		0%		0%		100.0%	
100	10.9		0.0		0.0		6.5		4.3		0.0		0.0		0.0			
101			---------------		---------------		---------------		---------------		---------------		---------------		---------------		---------------	
102	COLOMBIA		0%		0%		50%		0%		0%		50%		0%		100.0%	
103	247.1		0.0		0.0		123.6		0.0		0.0		123.6		0.0			
104			---------------		---------------		---------------		---------------		---------------		---------------		---------------		---------------	
105	JAMAICA		0%		10%		80%		10%		0%		0%		0%		100.0%	
106	224.1		0.0		22.4		179.3		22.4		0.0		0.0		0.0			
107			---------------		---------------		---------------		---------------		---------------		---------------		---------------		---------------	
108	MEXICO		0%		0%		0%		0%		50%		50%		0%		100.0%	
109	5818.7		0.0		0.0		0.0		0.0		2909.4		2909.4		0.0			
110			---------------		---------------		---------------		---------------		---------------		---------------		---------------		---------------	
111	Other		10%		10%		10%		10%		10%		50%		0%		100.0%	
112	3497.3		349.7		349.7		349.7		349.7		349.7		1748.7		0.0			
113			---------------		---------------		---------------		---------------		---------------		---------------		---------------		---------------	
114	Country 2		0%		0%		0%		0%		0%		0%		100%		100.0%	
115	0.0		0.0		0.0		0.0		0.0		0.0		0.0		0.0			
116			---------------		---------------		---------------		---------------		---------------		---------------		---------------		---------------	
117	The Baham		0%		0%		60%		40%		0%		0%		0%		100.0%	
118	471.2		0.0		0.0		282.7		188.5		0.0		0.0		0.0			
119			---------------		---------------		---------------		---------------		---------------		---------------		---------------		---------------	
120	Domin. Rep		0%		0%		60%		40%		0%		0%		0%		100.0%	
121	247.1		0.0		0.0		148.3		98.8		0.0		0.0		0.0			
122			---------------		---------------		---------------		---------------		---------------		---------------		---------------		---------------	
123	Country 5		0%		0%		0%		0%		0%		0%		100%		100.0%	
124	0.0		0.0		0.0		0.0		0.0		0.0		0.0		0.0			
125			---------------		---------------		---------------		---------------		---------------		---------------		---------------		---------------	
126																		
127	10516.39 (mt) into the U.S. before DOMESTIC seizures and after FOREIGN seizures.																	
128																		

Figure C.4—Distribution of Incoming Marijuana Among U.S. Entry Regions (cells A92 to R128)

Figure C.4 shows the next section of the marijuana transportation spreadsheet, MARITRAN.XLS. The user may decide on which of the six U.S. entry regions to send a country's marijuana. In the example shown, Mexico has 5,818.7 metric tons in cell A109, carried down from the previous table. In this example, the user has specified that 50 percent is shipped to the Southwest region (cell K108) and 50 percent is shipped the West region (cell M108).

	A	B	C	D	E	F	G	H	I	J	K	L	M	N
129														
130	TABLE 5A. DISTRIBUTION OF TRANSPORTATION MODES INTO U.S. ENTRY REGIONS													
131			*IN PERCENTS--DEFAULT TABLE*											
132			NORTH-		NORTH-		SOUTH-		SOUTH-		SOUTH-			
133			CENTRAL		EAST		EAST		CENTRAL		WEST		WEST	
134			---------		---------		---------		---------		---------		---------	
135	OMMERCIA		100%		45%		11%		8%		0%		1%	
136	AIR													
137														
138	PRIVATE		0%		0%		11%		0%		1%		0%	
139	AIR													
140														
141	OMMERCIA		0%		0%						17%		1%	
142	LAND						XXX		XXX					
143														
144	PRIVATE		0%		0%						77%		45%	
145	LAND						XXX		XXX					
146														
147	OMMERCIA		0%		54%		11%		16%		1%		12%	
148	SEA													
149														
150	PRIVATE		0%		1%		67%		75%		4%		40%	
151	SEA													
152														
153	CHECKSUM		100.0%		100.0%		100.0%		100.0%		100.0%		100.0%	
154														
155														
156	TABLE 5B. DISTRIBUTION OF TRANSPORTATION MODES INTO U.S. ENTRY REGIONS													
157			*IN PERCENTS--ALTERNATIVE TABLE*											
158	NOTE: The column percentage must equal 100%. Otherwise, none of the cell percentages in that col													
159			NORTH-		NORTH-		SOUTH-		SOUTH-		SOUTH-			
160			CENTRAL		EAST		EAST		CENTRAL		WEST		WEST	
161			---------		---------		---------		---------		---------		---------	
162	OMMERCIA		0%		0%		0%		0%		0%		0%	
163	AIR													
164														
165	PRIVATE		0%		0%		0%		0%		0%		0%	
166	AIR													
167														
168	OMMERCIA		0%		0%						0%		0%	
169	LAND						XXX		XXX					
170														
171	PRIVATE		0%		0%						0%		0%	
172	LAND						XXX		XXX					
173														
174	OMMERCIA		0%		0%		0%		0%		0%		0%	
175	SEA													
176														
177	PRIVATE		0%		0%		0%		0%		0%		0%	
178	SEA													
179														
180	TOTAL		NOT 100%		NOT 100%		NOT 100%		NOT 100%		NOT 100%		NOT 100%	
181														

Figure C.5—Distribution of Transportation Modes into U.S. Entry Regions (cells A129 to N181)

Figure C.5 shows the next section of the marijuana transportation spreadsheet, MARITRAN.XLS. The user may decide on the transportation modes of the marijuana into the six U.S. entry regions. In the example shown, 100 percent of the marijuana entering the North-Central region arrives through commercial air (cell C135). All of the percentages in Table 5A are derived automatically from seizure data in Table 6. Alternatively, the user can input other data in Table 5B. If any data are provided by the user in Table 5B, they will be used instead of the percentages in Table 5A. However, the user must ensure that the column percentages total 100 percent. Otherwise, none of the percentages in that column will be recognized by the model.

	A	B	C	D	E	F	G	H	I	J	K	L	M	N	O	P
182																
183	TABLE 6. SEIZURES OF Marijuana (TRANSPORTATION MODE BY U.S. ENTRY REGION)															
184							IN METRIC TONS									
185			NORTH-		NORTH-		SOUTH-		SOUTH-		SOUTH-				TOTAL	
186			CENTRAL		EAST		EAST		CENTRAL		WEST		WEST		BY MODE	
187	----------		----------		----------		----------		----------		----------		----------		----------	
188	OMMERCIA															
189	AIR		0.411		6.146		4.478		0.411		0.411		0.411		12.3	
190	----------		----------		----------		----------		----------		----------		----------		----------	
191	PRIVATE															
192	AIR		0.000		0.000		4.502		0.000		0.949		0.000		5.5	
193	----------		----------		----------		----------		----------		----------		----------		----------	
194	OMMERCIA															
195	LAND		0.000		0.000		---		---		16.015		0.222		16.2	
196	----------		----------		----------		----------		----------		----------		----------		----------	
197	PRIVATE															
198	LAND		0.000		0.000		---		---		72.840		13.040		85.9	
199	----------		----------		----------		----------		----------		----------		----------		----------	
200	OMMERCIA															
201	SEA		0.000		7.324		4.514		0.809		0.809		3.577		17.0	
202	----------		----------		----------		----------		----------		----------		----------		----------	
203	PRIVATE															
204	SEA		0.000		0.205		26.859		3.692		3.692		11.625		46.1	
205	----------		----------		----------		----------		----------		----------		----------		----------	
206	TOTAL														182.9	
207	BY REGION		0.4		13.7		40.4		4.9		94.7		28.9		182.9	
208																
209																

Figure C.6—Seizures of Marijuana (cells A182 to P209)

Figure C.6 shows the next section of the marijuana transportation spreadsheet, MARITRAN.XLS. The user must decide on the amount of marijuana that is seized *by entry region and transportation mode*. In the example shown, a total of 182.9 metric tons are seized (cell O206, O207). In the Northeast, for instance, 6.146 metric tons are seized by commercial air (cell E189), 7.324 by commercial sea (cell E201), and 0.205 via private sea (E204).

	A	B	C	D	E	F	G	H	I	J	K
1											
2					UNITED STATES DISTRIBUTION: MARIJUANA						
3					YEAR=		1991				
4											
5	TABLE 1.		MARIJUANA COMING INTO THE UNITED STATES								
6					BY REGION (MTs)						
7											
8			IMPORTED Marijuana								
9					Domestic				Alternate		
10			Net of Seizure		Production		TOTAL		TOTAL		
11	------------------		------------------		------------------		------------------		------------------		
12	NORTH-										
13	CENTRAL		349.3		1,400.0		1,749.3		#N/A		
14	------------------		------------------		------------------		------------------		------------------		
15	NORTH-										
16	EAST		358.5		0.0		358.5		#N/A		
17	------------------		------------------		------------------		------------------		------------------		
18	SOUTH-										
19	EAST		1,049.7		0.0		1,049.7		#N/A		
20	------------------		------------------		------------------		------------------		------------------		
21	SOUTH-										
22	CENTRAL		658.9		1,400.0		2,058.9		#N/A		
23	------------------		------------------		------------------		------------------		------------------		
24	SOUTH-										
25	WEST		3,164.4		1,400.0		4,564.4		#N/A		
26	------------------		------------------		------------------		------------------		------------------		
27											
28	WEST		4,752.7		1,400.0		6,152.7		#N/A		
29	------------------		------------------		------------------		------------------		------------------		
30							15,933.5		#N/A		
31	TOTAL		10,333.5		5,600.0		15,933.5				
32											
33											

Figure C.7—Marijuana Coming into the United States (cells A1 to K33)

Figure C.7 shows the first section of the marijuana U.S. distribution spreadsheet, MARIUSA.XLS. The user may input regional domestic production totals. There is also a column for the user to input an alternative total. In the example shown, 349.3 metric tons are coming into the North-Central region (after foreign and point of entry into the U.S. seizures), and is reflected in cell C13. The numbers in this column are linked to MARITRAN.XLS. The domestic production for the North Central region is 1,400 metric tons and is indicated in cell E13. Likewise, the user must specify all of the numbers in this column.

	A	B	C	D	E	F	G	H	I	J	K	L	M	N	O	P	Q	R	S	T
34	TABLE 2.		INTER-REGIONAL TRANSFERS OF Marijuana																	
35			(INPUT IN PERCENTS, CONVERTED TO METRIC TONS)																	
36					TRANSFER TO:															
37	TRANSFER		N. CENT		N. EAST		S. EAST		S. CENT		S. WEST		WEST		Transfers		Transfers		Amount	
38/39	FROM																			
40	N. CENTRAL		0%		0%		0%		0%		0%		0%		0%					
41		1,749.3	0.0		0.0		0.0		0.0		0.0		0.0		0.0		0.0		1749.3	
43	N. EAST		0%		0%		0%		0%		0%		0%		0%					
44		358.5	0.0		0.0		0.0		0.0		0.0		0.0		0.0		0.0		358.5	
46	S. EAST		0%		0%		0%		0%		0%		0%		0%					
47		1,049.7	0.0		0.0		0.0		0.0		0.0		0.0		0.0		0.0		1049.7	
49	S. CENTRAL		0%		0%		0%		0%		0%		0%		0%					
50		2,058.9	0.0		0.0		0.0		0.0		0.0		0.0		0.0		0.0		2058.9	
52	S. WEST		0%		0%		0%		0%		0%		0%		0%					
53		4,564.4	0.0		0.0		0.0		0.0		0.0		0.0		0.0		0.0		4564.4	
55	WEST		0%		0%		0%		0%		0%		0%		0%					
56		6,152.7	0.0		0.0		0.0		0.0		0.0		0.0		0.0		0.0		6152.7	
57																				
58																				
59																				

Figure C.8—Interregional Transfers of Marijuana (cells A34 to T59)

Figure C.8 shows the next section of the marijuana U.S. distribution spreadsheet, MARIUSA.XLS. The user may input interregional domestic transfers of marijuana. None are shown here, but would be placed in the cells within the matrix indicating a percentage (e.g., C43, C46, C49, C52, C55).

	A	B	C	D	E	F	G	H	I	J	K	L
60	TABLE 3.		STATE AND LOCAL SEIZURES									
61												
62	Gross Amount in each Region				--Minus--				Net Amount in each Region			
63	Ready for Sales (kgs.)				Seizures		Other		Ready for Sales (kgs.)			
64					(kgs.)		Losses					
65	N. CENTRAL		1,749,319		5397		0		1,743,922			
66	N. EAST		358,463		5397		0		353,066			
67	S. EAST		1,049,713		5397		0		1,044,316			
68	S. CENTRAL		2,058,901		5397		0		2,053,504			
69	S. WEST		4,564,365		5397		0		4,558,968			
70	WEST		6,152,689		5397		0		6,147,292			
71	TOTAL								TOTAL			
72			15,933,451		32,382		0		15,901,069			
73												
74												
75												
76	TABLE 4.		REGIONAL DISTRIBUTION OF NET MARIJUANA READY FOR SALES									
77			(INPUT IN PERCENTS, CONVERTED TO KILOGRAMS)									
78												
79	NORTH-CENTRAL											
80	CHICAGO (II)		0%		0							
81	DETROIT (II)		0%		0							
82	ALL OTHER		100%		1,743,922							
83												
84	NORTH-EAST											
85	BOSTON (II)		0%		0							
86	NEWARK (II)		0%		0							
87	NEW YORK (I)		0%		0							
88	ALL OTHER		100%		353,066							
89												
90	SOUTH-EAST											
91	ATLANTA		0%		0							
92	MIAMI (I)		0%		0							
93	ALL OTHER		100%		1,044,316							
94												
95	SOUTH-CENTRAL											
96	NEW ORLEANS		0%		0							
97	ALL OTHER		100%		2,053,504							
98												
99	SOUTH-WEST											
100	EL PASO (~I)		0%		0							
101	HOUSTON (I)		0%		0							
102	ALL OTHER		100%		4,558,968							
103												
104	WEST											
105	LOS ANGELES (I)		0%		0							
106	SAN DIEGO (II)		0%		0							
107	SAN FRANCISCO (II)		0%		0							
108	SEATTLE		0%		0							
109	ALL OTHER		100%		6,147,292							
110												
111	TOTAL				15,901,069							

Figure C.9—State and Local Seizures and the Regional Distribution of Net Marijuana Ready for Sale (cells A60 to L111)

Figure C.9 shows the next section of the marijuana U.S. distribution spreadsheet, MARIUSA.XLS. The user may input the amount of marijuana to be withdrawn from the system due to state and local seizures, and if desired, the amount of marijuana to ship to some major cities. Domestic seizures are withdrawn from the system by inputting values in cells E65 to E70. Also, other losses can be taken from the system in cells G65 to G70. If the user desires to allocate the marijuana to some major cities, this is accomplished by placing the percentage value in cells C80–81, C85–87, C91–92, C96, C100–101, and/or C105–108.

68

	A	B	C	D	E	F	G	H	I	J	K	L	M	N
112														
113	TABLE 5A. DRUG MARKET HIERARCHY--DEFAULT TABLE													
114					*IN KILOGRAMS PER ANNUM*									
115			NORTH-		NORTH-		SOUTH-		SOUTH-		SOUTH-			
116			CENTRAL		EAST		EAST		CENTRAL		WEST		WEST	
117	--------------		--------------		--------------		--------------		--------------		--------------		--------------	
118	Distributors		0.0		0.0		0.0		0.0		0.0		0.0	
119														
120			--------------		--------------		--------------		--------------		--------------		--------------	
121	Wholesalers		0.0		0.0		0.0		0.0		0.0		0.0	
122														
123	--------------		--------------		--------------		--------------		--------------		--------------		--------------	
124	Street Dealer		0.0		0.0		0.0		0.0		0.0		0.0	
125														
126			--------------		--------------		--------------		--------------		--------------		--------------	
127	USERS		0.122		0.122		0.122		0.122		0.122		0.122	
128														
129	--------------		--------------		--------------		--------------		--------------		--------------		--------------	
130														
131														
132	--------------		--------------		--------------		--------------		--------------		--------------		--------------	
133														
134														
135	TABLE 5B. DRUG MARKET HIERARCHY--ALTERNATIVE TABLE													
136					*IN KILOGRAMS PER ANNUM*									
137			NORTH-		NORTH-		SOUTH-		SOUTH-		SOUTH-			
138			CENTRAL		EAST		EAST		CENTRAL		WEST		WEST	
139	--------------		--------------		--------------		--------------		--------------		--------------		--------------	
140	Distributors		#N/A		#N/A		#N/A		#N/A		#N/A		#N/A	
141														
142	--------------		--------------		--------------		--------------		--------------		--------------		--------------	
143	Wholesalers		#N/A		#N/A		#N/A		#N/A		#N/A		#N/A	
144														
145	--------------		--------------		--------------		--------------		--------------		--------------		--------------	
146	Street Dealer		#N/A		#N/A		#N/A		#N/A		#N/A		#N/A	
147														
148	--------------		--------------		--------------		--------------		--------------		--------------		--------------	
149	USERS:		#N/A		#N/A		#N/A		#N/A		#N/A		#N/A	
150														
151	--------------		--------------		--------------		--------------		--------------		--------------		--------------	
152														
153														
154	--------------		--------------		--------------		--------------		--------------		--------------		--------------	
155														

Figure C.10—Drug Market Hierarchy Tables (cells A112 to N155)

Figure C.10 shows the next section of the marijuana U.S. distribution spreadsheet, MARIUSA.XLS. The user must input an estimate on the average amount of marijuana consumed. This figure shows only data for users, and indicates that 0.122 kg is an average value currently in the model. This is presented in cells C127, E127, G127, I127, K127, and M127. An alternative table, Table 5B, allows the user to input values too. If any values are placed in this table, they will be used instead of the ones in Table 5A. If the user desires alternative amounts of average use, these values can be input into cells C149, E149, G149, I149, K149, and M149.

TABLE 6. DRUG MARKET POPULATION DATA

	Distributor	Wholesaler	Street Dealers	USERS: (in 000s)	Population (in 000s)	Calculated Prevalence	Nat'l Household Survey Prevalence	RATIO
NORTH CENTRAL								
CHICAGO (II)	#DIV/0!	#DIV/0!	#DIV/0!	0	0	NA	9.2%	NA
DETROIT (II)	#DIV/0!	#DIV/0!	#DIV/0!	0	0	NA	9.2%	NA
ALL OTHER	#DIV/0!	#DIV/0!	#DIV/0!	14,294	58,031	24.6%	9.4%	2.62
NORTHEAST								
BOSTON (II)	#DIV/0!	#DIV/0!	#DIV/0!	0	0	NA	10.0%	NA
NEWARK (II)	#DIV/0!	#DIV/0!	#DIV/0!	0	0	NA	10.0%	NA
NEW YORK (I)	#DIV/0!	#DIV/0!	#DIV/0!	0	0	NA	10.0%	NA
ALL OTHER	#DIV/0!	#DIV/0!	#DIV/0!	2,894	47,152	6.1%	9.9%	0.62
SOUTHEAST								
ATLANTA	#DIV/0!	#DIV/0!	#DIV/0!	0	0	NA	8.6%	NA
MIAMI (I)	#DIV/0!	#DIV/0!	#DIV/0!	0	0	NA	8.6%	NA
ALL OTHER	#DIV/0!	#DIV/0!	#DIV/0!	8,560	30,996	27.6%	8.6%	3.21
SOUTH CENTRAL								
NEW ORLEANS	#DIV/0!	#DIV/0!	#DIV/0!	0	0	NA	8.6%	NA
ALL OTHER	#DIV/0!	#DIV/0!	#DIV/0!	16,832	14,860	113.3%	8.6%	13.17
SOUTHWEST								
EL PASO (-)	#DIV/0!	#DIV/0!	#DIV/0!	0	0	NA	8.6%	NA
HOUSTON (I)	#DIV/0!	#DIV/0!	#DIV/0!	0	0	NA	8.6%	NA
ALL OTHER	#DIV/0!	#DIV/0!	#DIV/0!	37,369	19,900	187.8%	9.2%	20.36
WEST								
LOS ANGELES (I)	#DIV/0!	#DIV/0!	#DIV/0!	0	0	NA	11.7%	NA
SAN DIEGO (II)	#DIV/0!	#DIV/0!	#DIV/0!	0	0	NA	11.7%	NA
SAN FRANCISCO (II)	#DIV/0!	#DIV/0!	#DIV/0!	0	0	NA	11.7%	NA
SEATTLE	#DIV/0!	#DIV/0!	#DIV/0!	0	0	NA	11.7%	NA
ALL OTHER	#DIV/0!	#DIV/0!	#DIV/0!	50,388	30,193	166.9%	11.7%	14.26
US TOTAL	#DIV/0!	#DIV/0!	#DIV/0!	130,337	201,131	64.8%	9.6%	

Figure C.11—Drug Market Population Data (cells A156 to T195)

Figure C.11 shows the last section of the marijuana U.S. distribution spreadsheet, MARIUSA.XLS. The user must ensure that the population numbers presented in column M are basically correct. These figures are based on 1990 census data. The estimated number of users is presented in column I. These percentages are compared to the population numbers in column M to obtain the calculated prevalence percentage shown in column O. This percentage can be compared to the National Household Survey percentage presented in column Q. Finally, the ratio in column S is the ratio of the model's calculated prevalence to the Household Survey's estimated prevalence.

D. A Short Primer on the INCSR's Data-Collection Methodology

In this appendix, we present a verbatim portion of the 1991 *International Narcotics Control Strategy Report* that discusses the methodology for estimating various factors in illegal drug production. It identifies the estimates in which there is the least (and most) certainty, as well as some of the reasons for the differentials in certainty.[1] This discussion is applicable to cocaine, heroin, and marijuana.

Methodology for Estimating Illegal Drug Production: How much do we know? This report [1991 INCSR] contains tables showing a variety of illicit narcotics-related data. While these numbers represent the United States Government's (USG) best effort to sketch the dimensions of the international drug problem, the reader should be aware that the picture is not always as precise as we would like it to be. The numbers range from cultivation figures, hard data derived by proven means, to crop production and drug yield estimates, where many more variables come into play. Since much information is lacking where yields are concerned, the numbers are subject to revision as more data becomes known.

What we know with reasonable certainty: The most reliable information we have on illicit drugs is how many hectares are under cultivation. For more than a decade, the USG has estimated the extent of illicit cultivation in a dozen nations using proven methods similar to those used to estimate the size of licit crops at home and abroad. We can thus estimate the size of crops with reasonable accuracy.

What we know with less certainty: Where crop yields are concerned, the picture is less clear. How much of a finished product a given area will produce is difficult to estimate, since small changes in such factors as soil fertility, weather, farming techniques, and disease can produce widely varying results from year to year and place to place. In addition, most illicit drug crop areas are inaccessible to the USG, making scientific information difficult to obtain. Moreover, we must stress that even as we refine our methods of analysis, we are estimating *potential* crop available for harvest. These estimates do not allow for losses, which could represent anything from a tenth to a third (or more) of a crop in some areas for some harvests. Thus, the estimate of the potential

---

[1]Refer to the *International Narcotics Control Strategy Report*, United States, Department of State, March 1991, pp. 7–8.

crop is useful in providing comparative analysis from year to year, but the actual quantity of final product remains elusive.

Harvest Estimates: Estimating the quantities of coca leaf, opium gum, and marijuana actually harvested and available for processing into finished narcotics remains a major challenge. *We currently cannot accurately estimate this amount for any illicit crop in any nation.* While farmers naturally have strong incentives to maximize their harvests of what is almost always their most profitable cash crop, the harvest depends upon the efficiency of farming practices and the wastage caused by poor practices or difficult weather conditions during and after harvest. A tenth to a third (or more) of a crop may be lost in some areas during harvests. Additional information and analysis may enable us to make adjustments for these factors in the future. Similar deductions for local consumption of unprocessed coca leaf and opium may be possible as well through the accumulation of additional information and research.

Processing Estimates. The wide variation in processing efficiencies achieved by traffickers complicates the task of estimating the quantity of cocaine or heroin which could be refined from a crop. These efficiencies vary because of differences in the origin and quality of the raw material used, the technical processing method employed, the size and sophistication of laboratories, and the skill and experience of local workers and chemists. The USG continues to estimate potential cocaine production as a range based on processing efficiencies that appear to be most common.

The actual amount of dry coca leaf or opium converted into a final product during any time period remains unknown, given the possible losses noted earlier. There are indications, however, that cocaine processing efficiencies improved during the 1980s, and that traffickers still have considerable room for improvement.

Figures will change as techniques and data quality improve. The reader may ask: are this year's figures definitive? The reply is, almost certainly, some are not. Additional research may result in future revision to USG estimates of potential drug production. For the present, however, these statistics represent the state of the art. As the art improves, so will the precision of the estimates.

E. A Simulation to Test for the Effect of Propagating Errors in the Model

Because of the high number of parameters in the model and the likelihood that most are estimated with some degree of error, there is the possibility that even slight errors in parameter values can propagate throughout the system and translate into large errors in the later stages of the model. We conducted a simulation to test the model's robustness in the face of these propagating errors. We chose six parameters and randomly changed each by an amount within 20 percent of the initial value.[1] Then, we compared the model's estimated number of users from each of the 50 iterations to the model's beginning value.[2]

The six parameters are taken from each of the model's spreadsheets (i.e., production, transportation, and domestic distribution) and are representative of all of the model's parameters in terms of their impact on the model's output. In other words, some parameters have a large influence on the model's output, while others have relatively little impact. The six parameters are

- Mexico Production Factor (metric tons of marijuana per hectare)—Mexico constitutes nearly 88 percent of the estimated hectares of marijuana under cultivation for 1991.[3] The sensitivity analysis presented in Table 4.1 reveals that this parameter exercises a significant impact on the model's output. For example, a 50-percent change in this parameter results in an 18.3-percent change in the estimated number of users.

- Mexico Consumption (metric tons)—Approximately 100 metric tons were consumed in Mexico during 1991, making it the largest domestic consumer of marijuana among the four producing countries included in the model. However, the sensitivity analysis reveals that this parameter has an insignificant influence on the model's output. A 50-percent change in this parameter resulted in a 0.2-percent change in the estimated number of users.

---

[1]We used Excel's random number generator to create a table of random numbers that ranged in value from –20 percent to +20 percent. The 20 percent figure is somewhat arbitrary, but we believe an appropriate amount for this illustrative exercise.

[2]Any propagating errors would ostensibly find their greatest impact at the end of the model, so we decided to use the estimated number of users, because it is the final model estimate.

[3]This includes Mexico, Colombia, Jamaica, and Belize.

- Foreign Seizures (metric tons)—With only around 8 metric tons of marijuana removed from the system, this parameter has a negligible impact on the model's output. The sensitivity analysis confirmed this when a 50-percent change in the parameter resulted in a 0.03-percent change in the estimated number of users.

- Production from "Other" (metric tons)—About 3,500 metric tons of marijuana were produced from "other" sources in 1991, which constitutes approximately 27 percent of the total production accounted for in the model. Consequently, this parameter can have a major influence over the model's output.

- Domestic Seizures (metric tons)—Since only about 32 metric tons of marijuana were extracted from the system in 1991, this parameter has a minor effect on the model's output. Again, the sensitivity analysis confirmed this when a 50-percent change in the parameter resulted in a 0.6-percent change in the estimated number of users.

- Annual Consumption (kilograms)—This parameter can potentially have a major effect on the model's output. The sensitivity analysis shows that a 50-percent change in its value results in a 33-percent change in the estimated number of users, which is a rather substantial effect.

The output from the simulation is presented in Table E.1. The beginning value in the model for the estimated number of users is 130.3 million.[4] The minimum value obtained is 101.2 million (or 77.7 percent of the beginning value); the

Table E.1

Output from the Simulation

Iteration	Users (000)	Iter.	Users (000)	Iter.	Users (000)	Iter.	Users (000)	Iter.	Users (000)
1	155,861	11	153,221	21	129,393	31	110,075	41	155,504
2	163,724	12	115,039	22	154,202	32	128,629	42	133,627
3	168,206	13	131,187	23	130,005	33	143,553	43	103,822
4	129,617	14	135,300	24	135,458	34	102,580	44	143,778
5	123,954	15	138,818	25	138,415	35	158,065	45	119,246
6	113,251	16	158,066	26	141,126	36	148,500	46	119,039
7	127,158	17	130,698	27	138,409	37	126,332	47	141,817
8	164,233	18	115,709	28	101,241	38	154,636	48	125,661
9	117,587	19	132,595	29	128,780	39	141,424	49	114,981
10	131,846	20	142,525	30	110,090	40	166,493	50	148,535

---

[4]One should not interpret this as our definitive estimate of the number of marijuana users in the United States. Rather, it should be interpreted as the number of users there must be *if one accepts all previous parameter estimates in the model.*

maximum is 168.2 million (129.1 percent of the beginning value); the median is 133.1 million (102.1 percent of the beginning value); and the mean is 134.8 million (103.5 percent of the beginning value).

These data are largely clustered around the beginning value. This is evidenced by the fact that 92 percent of the simulation output is within 25 percent of the beginning value, as illustrated in Figure E.1.

Moreover, these data are more or less uniformly distributed around the beginning value. This is illustrated in Figure E.2.

We conclude from this simulation that the model is generally robust in the face of propagating errors. The vast majority of the simulation outputs fall close to the beginning value of 130.3 million. Indeed, 92 percent of the simulation output fall within 25 percent of the beginning value. In a limited number of cases, however, the effect of propagating errors produces values that are significantly different from the beginning value. All of this suggests that in most cases (but not all) the errors will countervail each other.

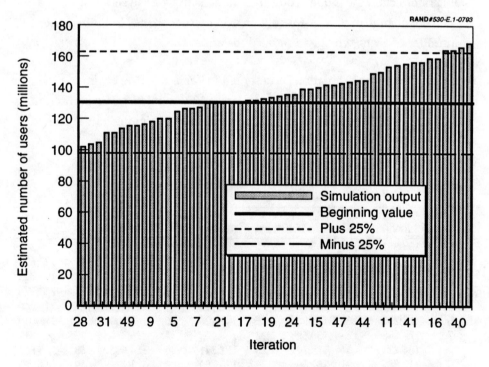

Figure E.1—Fifty Random Changes in Six Marijuana Parameters: 92 Percent of Simulation Output Is Within 25 Percent of the Beginning Value

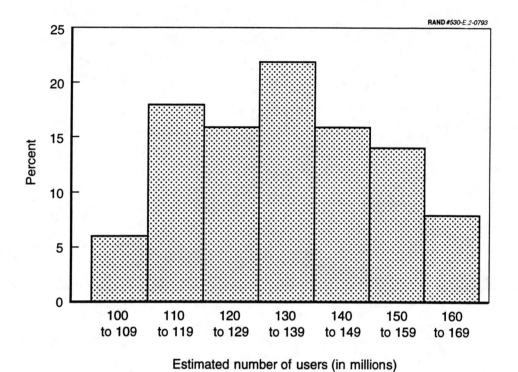

Figure E.2—Histogram of Marijuana User Output

Bibliography

Abt Associates, *What America's Users Spend On Illegal Drugs*, A Technical Paper for ONDCP, June 1991.

Carpenter, Ted G., and R. Channing Rouse, "Perilous Panacea: The Military in the Drug War," a CATO Institute Policy Analysis, No. 128, February 15, 1990.

Childress, Michael, *A System Description of the Heroin Trade*, MR-234-A/DPRC, forthcoming.

Dombey-Moore, Bonnie, Susan Resetar, and Michael Childress, *A System Description of the Cocaine Trade*, MR-236-A/AF, RAND, forthcoming.

INSCR, see U.S. Department of State.

Kleiman, Mark A. R., *Marijuana: Costs of Abuse, Costs of Control*, New York: Greenwood Press, 1989.

National Narcotics Consumers Committee, *National Narcotics Intelligence Consumers Committee Report*, various years.

Perl, Raphael F., *Drug Control: International Policy and Options*, Congressional Research Service, Issue Brief, September 21, 1989.

Reuter, Peter, "The Economic Significance of Illegal Markets in the United States: Some Observations," *Economics and Lavoro*, Vol. XVIII, No. I, pp. 135–142.

Reuter, Peter, and David Ronfeldt, *Quest for Integrity: The Mexican-U.S. Drug Issue in the 1980s*, RAND, N-3266-USDP, 1992.

Richburg, Keith B., "Reagan Order Defines Drug Trade as Security Threat," *Washington Post*, June 8, 1986.

Surrett, William Roy, *The International Narcotics Trade: An Overview of Its Dimensions, Production Sources, and Organizations*, Congressional Research Service, October 3, 1988.

Treaster, Joseph B., "Costly and Scarce, Marijuana Is a High More Are Rejecting," *New York Times*, October 29, 1991.

U.S. Congress, House Committee on the Judiciary, *Posse Comitatus Act, Hearing*, 97th Congress, 1st Session, June 3, 1981.

U.S. Department of Defense, *Defense Science Board Summer Study on Detection and Neutralization of Illegal Drugs and Terrorist Devices*, October 13, 1987.

U.S. Department of Health and Human Services, National Institute on Drug Abuse (NIDA), *National Household Survey on Drug Abuse: Population Estimates*, various issues.

U.S. Department of Health and Human Services, News Release, December 19, 1991.

U.S. Department of Justice, Drug Enforcement Administration, Office of Intelligence, *From the Source to the Street: Mid-1990 Prices for Cannabis, Cocaine, and Heroin, Intelligence Trends*, various issues.

U.S. Department of State, Bureau of International Narcotics Matters, *International Narcotics Control Strategy Report*, various issues.

U.S. General Accounting Office, *Drug Law Enforcement: Military Assistance for Anti-Drug Agencies*, GAO/GGD-88-27, December 1987.

U.S. Office of National Drug Control Policy, *National Drug Control Strategy: Implementing the President's Plan*, various issues.

Warner, Roger, *Invisible Hand: The Marijuana Business*, New York: Beech Tree Books, 1986.